WHEN THE GODDESS CALLS

2ND EDITION

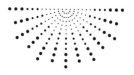

TINA PAVLOU

AND CO.

Disclaimer:

Although the author(s) have tried to recreate events, locales and conversations from their memories of them. In order to maintain their anonymity in some instances they may have changed the names of individuals and places, they may have changed some identifying characteristics and details such as physical properties, occupations and places of residence.

Although the author(s) and publisher have made every effort to ensure that the information in this book was correct at press time, the author(s) and publisher do not assume and hereby disclaim any liability to any party for any loss, damage, or disruption caused by errors or omissions, whether such errors or omissions result from negligence, accident, or any other cause.

This book is not intended as a substitute for the medical advice of physicians. The reader should regularly consult a physician in matters relating to his/her health and particularly with respect to any symptoms that may require diagnosis or medical attention.

CONTENTS

1

TINA PAVLOU

*G*lastonbury is the heart chakra of the world. In fact it is the heart chakra of the universe, some say the multi-verse but to me it is my sanctuary, a place where my heart and mind healed, a place where I found me.

The energy there is so magical, let me explain why Glaston-bury/Avalon is my second home. I first visited Glastonbury with a friend Abbey, five years ago to attend a dragon workshop with the amazing Hay House Author, Tim Wilde who I now consider as a friend.

Abbey and I did not know what to expect all we knew was that we had to go, so we booked into a healing waters retreat and off we drove early in the morning . After a four hour drive, as we approached we sensed the energy around us becoming softer and more gentle.

We arrived in Glastonbury totally blown away the whole place had a quirkiness, you could feel the magic, the Avalon magic, King Arthurs magic I felt the medieval energy and it felt like home. It was utterly overwhelming.

That weekend changed our spiritual paths and opened us up to a higher consciousness . We witnessed cloud formations change shape over the Tor through the power of our group thoughts and consciousness, and I witnessed magic and felt love in my heart, and I fell in love with Avalon.

Today Glastonbury/Avalon is a powerful energetic centre and pilgrims of all faiths are drawn to the energy of the town and the surrounding areas which include Stonehenge the masculine energy, and Avebury the feminine energy.

They are drawn to the crystal shops, the many tarot readers, they come for massages and healings, or to visit spiritual bookshops. Some come to join in ceremonies in the sacred places of Avalon on top of the Tor at Chalice Well, in the Goddess temple, in the Goddess house or at the Shek-inaashram and not forgetting in the presence of the 9 mogens.

9 sisters who are the feminine in nature, they are the feminine Goddesses who are called by Thitis, Slitom, Thetis, Gliten, Glitoena, Moronoe, Mazoe, Tyronoe and Morgen Le Fey and the Lady of Avalon whose name is Nolava.

The veil to Avalon was raised to hide its mysteries from the eyes of the non-believers the sacred isle disappeared into the mists of our forgetting, leaving the red blood spring and the white blood spring as the only things that continued to flow.

Legend has it that Jesus' Disciple Joseph of Arimathea arrived in Avalon and planted the Hawn Thorn Tree. King Arthur and Gwenhwyfar (Guinevere) fell in love in Avalon, and the greatest most famous story by far is that of Merlin.

Merlin was a wizard which is the title for the head Druid masculine, but being known as Merlin is ages old and is considered to be an Atlantean wizard who has had many incarnations and is extraordinarily long lived.

In each of these incarnations Merlin was present in Atlantis, Egypt and Avalon and is guiding us now. Merlin is a guardian and works very closely with those he has incarnated or had a life with, and I am very blessed as Merlin works closely with me. I have many pictures taken at Tintagel Cornwall, in Merlin's cave where you can actually see the blue energy, these are on my Facebook page if you would like to view them.

I have had many visitations from Merlin, and he will often step in to assist me with healing clients, his energy mirrors that of the gentleness of the Dalai Lama. Merlin can be felt all around Glastonbury especially at the bottom of the Tor in the White Waters which is the Spring underneath the Tor where you can bathe in Avalon healing waters.

This is also the entrance to the fairy realm you can visit most days but be careful what you wish for because your wishes will be granted. Outside running in the streets are two springs and two wells a white water well and a red water well one representing the masculine and one representing the feminine.

Do Fairies Exist?

They live on a different vibration they live on the second plane, but I will save my fairy stories for another chapter.

At the foot of the Tor is the Shikenham Ashram, the first time I entered I walked into the temple and sat down for a fire ceremony and Kirtian I was hooked and was in awe as I was cleansed . We sang and chanted mantras it was a feeling of peace, calm and joy like my sole had been searching for this and I was finally home.

This was the beginning of my love affair with Glastonbury. After that I just could not get enough, I travelled back there as much as I could just to be in this magical healing land and each time I visited I would have the most epic visions and received messages and witnessed magic with my own eyes.

One day I went to see the Sharman called Kestrel at the Bridget Healing Centre in the court yard. I was totally blown away, the healing I received showed my ancestors and the parts of my linage that needed healing.

I felt like I was taken to another timeline where I meet Rhiannon one of the Avalon Priestesses and I saw myself as a young lady in Medieval time living there and I saw myself with a soul mate who I recognised in his timeline too.

The Goddesses reactivated sacred knowledge in me that day. I know that I have had an incarnation in Avalon, and I saw who I was this is why all the tales, the magic, the stories and the energies are familiar to me. I know all that is happening now, I now know that timelines separate realities and dimensions simultaneously.

To explain this to you about 7 years ago I had a dream, a dream that was so real I was in a white corridor with lots of white doors as I walked down the corridor I opened one of the doors and entered and I was in Edwardian times, I became a little scared and went to leave as I tried to open the door it vanished and I heard a voice say, "you have a lesson still to learn in this lifetime" and then I woke up.

That day I went for a healing session with my holistic practitioner, I told her what I had seen in my dream and she smiled at me and said, "have you read the book 'One' written by Richard Bach" I said no, she told me to read it. I was so eager to read it that when I left, I went onto YouTube to see if there was an audio version and I found one, a version a woman was reading.

I went down to the beach and listened and was blown away by what I heard, as he too had been in the white corridor and saw the white doors and he had entered more than one door and they were all different life times and different lives and different versions of him.

Explanation ...... you see we are all living simultaneous lives, multiple lives on multiple time lines at once How amazing is that!!!!

That means my timeline is happening now in Glastonbury with the Lady of Avalon with all the Goddesses and priestesses so that also means that the knowledge and downloads that I am receiving are from that timeline and source .

This is where I get excited this is when I know that I am on my divine timing lifepath helping thousands of people and these people could be helping me on different timelines. This is karmic this is conscious awareness . So, if this is happening now all we have to do is make sure we love because this will triple across all timelines and dimensions.

I have now decided to share this love and knowledge I have discovered and have set up my Goddess retreats for all to feel the magic.

My Retreats are sold out in days without even advertising, this is where I 'birthed' my books, my ideas, the Goddess rooms, my future business this is where my downloads come in so sharp so acute and accurate this is where the magic happens. I sit on this ancient land and I listen to the knowledge the elders want me to share with the world.

My mind is unlike most, I see and hear (clairvoyantly) all through the day and all through the night. I am always writing in my journal, all the ideas gifted to me. The night dreams are the hardest, as let's be honest here, I do just want to sleep, I find it tough seeing negative things I wake up with anxiety knowing something rubbish will happen.

I work with Angel numbers and during my dreams at night I am shown sets of numbers. This is a guide for me how the next few days will pan out.

For example, 11.11 means my thoughts are manifesting so keep them bright and focused.

22.22 means wishes coming true

33.33 a big fat yes meaning the masters are with me

44.44 my most dreaded number means something not so nice will happen and waking up is not nice as my mind goes wild knowing something bad will happen even though I have my Angels surrounding me.

55.55 means positive outcome and change

66.66 means work and career

777 means miracles, my favourite

888 shows abundance

999 new beginnings

000 full circle

My gift is to feel and read energy from anywhere around the globe. I work from a place of creation and love and are blessings, to be able to see and hear truth. Glastonbury portals enhance my gifts and encourage my inner child to come out to play, especially in the world of mystery of magic and fairy tales, which by the way is my truth .

I have been on many courses and learnt many healing modalities which I call my spiritual tool box. Ask me what I specialise in and I will say as an intuitive healer but once again in the portals of love, Avalon magnifies all of my gifts.

How do I keep my vibration high????

I have stopped drinking alcohol as it lowers my frequencies and I would quite often have waywards or entities around me, you see what people don't realise is that every 'spirit' drink has an actual spirit entity attached to it, and most people who drink a lot or binge drink have these pesky things attached to them to and then wonder why they are up and down unable to think properly and feel drained and it is because of this.

For example, one Saturday afternoon my friend and I where sat on the London tube when a very unhealthy man boarded the train, standing next to him was, how I can only describe as a weird looking male a bit like Beetle Juice (if you remember that film). He pulled a face at us, so we just looked at each other and went into a Theta State and sent the wayward to the light.

Waywards are people who have passed over who were too afraid to go to the light and are still wandering around, you may call them ghosts. I make sure that I have holistic treatments every week to keep my vibrations and frequency high and clean. I bless my food and keep it plant based, I avoid meat dairy and processed foods. Everything has an energy and high vibrational food enters my body.

I listen to audio books daily to fill my brain with knowledge that I choose and not random media, so I avoid television and radio but I do allow myself to listen to high frequency music on YouTube.

528HZ miracle tones to bring positive transformation and all 9 solfeggio frequency's for full body aura cleanse and the best sounds to heal and sleep to are 432HZ Angelic and healing tones.

When I read, I like to digest truth one of my go to bibles is The Secret Language of your Body by Inna Segal and anything by the medical medium Anthony William.

I have to nurture and take care of my spirit my beautiful mind and my divine feminine body especially emotions. My emotions and senses are very heightened and as an empath I feel everything. Being a clear channel, I am able to connect with source/creator or whatever word you like to use. Every person on this planet has the potential to live in this frequency but as I see with humans there is so much work to be done.

People operate from their emotions and not from the heart. I see this on a day to day basis I see people acting out their mother issues, their wounded child. Yes, we can add empathy and sympathy for them but ultimately they must take responsibility for their own lives. Yes, healing is hard. Yes it is scary, but what is the alternative drink? Drugs? Bad behaviour? Searching, searching, searching.

At the Goddess rooms in Ramsgate our Love Hub my nickname for our beautiful place . We help hundreds of souls from all walks of life and since June of this year 2019 there has been a huge increase in the number of people coming for healing who are suddenly having their physic gifts opening up.

I understand more than most what deep deep pain is and realising the eons of lifetimes of emotions fear, anxiety and stress has been the greatest gift to myself every negative emotion if not dealt with can manifest into an illness and there is no way that I would allow another's bad behaviour towards me affect my body or health.

The Goddess retreats are now running in Glastonbury, Bali, Egypt the lands of the Goddesses. You are taught all that I have written and more how to embrace your feminine energy and how to align you best life how to connect you heart and womb and rediscover your lost magic and truly love yourself.

I am so excited and so thrilled to be able to tell you in this chapter that magic and miracles are real. One day I hope you can join us and become and author in one of The Goddess Calls books so that your story can be shared around the world and will assist others with their life too. After all your life is so sacred your gifts are unique . Thank you for joining The Goddess Calls movement.

Love Tina

Who lives happily ever after

AUTHOR BIO

TINA PAVLOU

Tina Pavlou is a Clairvoyant and an intuitive Coach and Mentor.. a seer into the Spiritual realms, who works with the Seven Planes of Existence and the Spiritual Laws; a Theta Healer Instuctor, an Angelic Reiki Master and teacher, a Suara Sound Therapist and a Divine FEMININE Taoism Sexual Energy Teacher from Kent in England.

Tina specialises in empowering people to live their best lives by giving them the spiritual tools to do so.

After experiencing the Dark Night of the Soul, she made it her passion to help as many people as she could, so they would never have to experience as much suffering and pain as she had.

It is impossible to be around Tina without feeling anything other than positivity and love as she vibrates on such a Divine, Goddess high frequency. Her passion is just love.

CONTACT DETAILS

EMAIL: Pavloutina@yahoo.co.uk

WEBSITE: tinapavlou.com

facebook.com/tinapavlouangellady

instagram.com/tina_pavlou_angel_lady_

2

ANNA TOKAROVA

*L*ove - a lot has been written and said on the subject since the beginning of time and this chapter will be my contribution of thoughts and observations so far in my life's journey. Love and light and joy and in we go.

I was brought up in (what I grew up to believe) a 'traditional' family. From early childhood (and I remember events from as early as 6 months to the horror of my parents) I had a deep awareness that I was loved by my parents. It was more of an awareness rather than a feeling. I could see how much and how hard they tried to do everything for my wellbeing. Sometimes their ideas of what was best for me were very humorous.

For instance, they would try to keep me fit and active by asking me to act as a remote control for the very old TV set we used to have (yes that's right the big box looking one). At home, there was always fun, joy and support. My parents were great at making sure I did not have a care in the world, and I will always love them for the warmth, stability and support they were able to offer me over the years.

They were very different people united by their own unique 'Love', the story that came with it and some common goals. As a child, I enjoyed observing how they expressed love and it was very different at various stages of their lives.

My experiences, witnessing and observations have shaped my opinions and perceptions. It took me a while to understand and work out who I am and what is true to me. I believe it's a lifelong process actually and takes us a lifetime. We get to see, feel, experience different expressions of emotion and love.

Helen was a friend from childhood days that I am still in touch with, a dear soul sister, who once taught me an invaluable lesson. She was top of the class in our year, a straight-A student and I thought her relationship with her parents must be ideal. Mine was good but I had the odd lower grades and was always told to make sure not to repeat the pattern by my family.

So, one day I gathered up the courage, as Helen was very tough back in the days, and asked her how amazing it must be to never have anything to be told off about. She was laughing so hard and said after, that I had no idea what it's like to be always good at studies. Helen continued that with any person you could always find something to tell them off about. Back then I was shocked and in disbelief.

Her life looked so perfect on the outside and she did have an amazing family caring for her, but we never fully know what happens in another person's world, heart and soul. I realised never to jump to conclusions and even the best of us have issues or things to work on.

Coming back to family life in my early days there were plenty of lessons to be learnt. I was blessed throughout my life up to the present day to have very good teachers. Think about it, what were your teachers like? At home, at school, among friends, colleagues and lovers?

Being a libra sign I always feel the need to balance out people, the environment around me and situations. At one point I was even resentful of my zodiac sign. The thought in my mind would be along the line that it's somehow out of my control and my innate nature not to act in my best interest but always put other's interests first. I can tell you right away that is no way to live.

It's very hard to find yourself if your consciousness is swarmed with thoughts of others, how are they feeling in their shoes, and what to do to make everyone happy. It took me a long while to learn this, way longer than I hoped it would. Even now, I am still learning but a bit better now and am very happy about it.

I have created the most outlandish situations in my life. Some of them so outrageous that I think if I were to put them on paper it would spontaneously combust. Yes, that bad or worse. All to learn love. I leant that love has many forms and expressions. Everyone has a different definition of it.

What love is to me is unlikely to be the same love to you or anyone else. For a very long time, love equated for me with sacrifice. Oh boy .... was I good at 'love'? With this concept not only did I 'sacrifice' myself for others but also expected it in return, as this was my only understanding of it. Subsequently, that led to quite a few messed up relationships and subsequently marriage ending in divorce.

It was how the story and program have been playing out in my head and life. The trauma that I put myself through at times was just about bearable. I took everything very close to heart and struggled to understand when my grandmother used to tell to look at situations in life through a prism and from a distance. Looking at all of my 'only loves' and 'loves for life' I just smile or mostly laugh and am filled with gratitude and lightness in my heart.

Having created amazing scenarios, I am lucky to look back at all the amazing adventures and experiences I've had. They allowed me to practice being me, the different me that I can be. They supported me when I needed it and dissolved when no longer required.

That is so fascinating is it not? Embracing choice and role in the events and situations that happen in life, at the same time recognising and respecting the roles and choices of others. Being an empath can be fun and interesting if we choose and allow it to be so. I used to choose more pain and suffering as the dominating thought in my mind was better I suffer, and my family stays blissfully happy.

The result was not pretty: feelings of despair overwhelmed me most of the time. At one point I even kept a horror journal. Things I would not share with anyone but were too tough to hold in, I would spill them out on paper. That helped to release some of the pain.

After a while, I discovered a different way of self-love. I would write the opposite of what happened in the day. It worked like magic. The stories on those pages were so happy it was infectious in the most beautiful of ways. Then I decided to integrate it into my speech. It took effort but I saw results. Perception and focus are everything. Happy solutions to situations started coming my way. I use the method to date when tricky situations occur. It's a different way of living for me, others and the situations I am engaged in.

At this point, you are probably thinking I have everything sorted out in my life. I have realised having more faith helps, believing there is always a better way if you are not happy with the one you think you are dealt, choosing responsibly over victimhood. I frequently get stuck in my mind and the paradigms I create.

The difference now is that I know I can increase them if I choose to. If I feel provoked, threatened or in any way stressed I am aware I need to breathe, find my balance and then look at the situation instead of immediately reacting to circumstances. I can be overly dramatic and passionate. If I feel something is serious to me, I can easily go from 0 to 100 in a nanosecond, which is not the healthiest way to experience an emotion. Impatience was another vice close to my heart.

Result-driven culture can drive anyone desperate. It took an 8 year-long divorce to teach me that patience is the virtue to have handy on standby.

Originally when I was thinking about what to write about, I wanted to write on the topic of getting through abusive relationships. As I was doing more research and thinking more about it, I realised that firstly, a lot is already written on the subject. Secondly, it's sad and there's plenty of sadness as it is without me adding to it. Thirdly, my intention is for this piece to be useful and joyful to you reader. In my relationships, I have observed and seen that the same people can be very different with different people. I was the same and different at the same time, in all my friendships and relationship.

It's an exchange of energy and information. We react to what we receive, and people react to what we project. So, as I have worked on myself, and discovered more of me and how my mind works I have seen the dynamics of my relationships with other people adjust accordingly. Healthier personal boundaries, recognition of my values and priorities, learning to stand up for myself and my ideas in constructive ways, dealing with conflict (which, being a Libra I used to avoid at all cost and learnt the hard way - conflict is part of life, creation and growth).

The biggest part was to accept what I felt were mistakes. They were all my choices and I now love my mistakes. They are my creation and allow me access to new information, knowledge and skills I did not have before. For example, I was always highly scared of criticism. I still am to be honest just different, and to a lesser degree.

My fear of not appearing perfect at certain points of my life was very interesting. Only over time, I realised that criticism came regardless of the appearances we keep or actions we take, which makes it even more crucial to stay authentic to yourself and follow your own path.

Quite often now I avoid taking on new projects from the knowledge and experience of past ones that felt like blood, tears and exhaustingly hard work. That was my choice and creation then, what else can I create now? I felt strongly about a more comprehensive way of healing and therapy.

When people came for treatments, I was happy to help and see that people cared enough to love themselves in this form of self-care. The only thing was I could only help one person at a time, and the biggest cost to me was my health, energy and time. I wanted to help, inspire and empower more people to look after themselves and their families.

The best way ahead for me has been self-care and taking breaks for thoughtful pause. I have created a lot of tricky situations by overworking to the point there was little time for constructive thought. In my personal dictionary rest equated with laziness, and if I dared to rest, punishment of some kind would soon follow. A very similar pattern followed with happiness. I had to pay for moments of joy with long times of sadness as if it was another form of punishment and joy has been a wrongdoing of some kind.

The result was a very overworked, mostly sad Anna... that created a whole bunch of unforeseen at the time, side effects. Exhaustion for one, both physical and mental. I got to a point I could not lift a finger even if you were to dangle a million pounds in front of me. I was so tired that even rest felt like hard work and seemed like it required more effort than it was worth, so I would go back to working even harder because that was the only thing I knew how to do well.

My thoughts at the time were at least I was doing something I was good at and contributing to people's wellness. My family and personal life suffered as I did not know how to love myself or them. So, I chose to avoid addressing those parts of life altogether. It's tricky to do catch up now. When it was happening, I knew I would regret it, but I also knew that at that time I did not know any better, and I eventually forgave myself.

With more knowledge and options that I see now, I try to find ways of rest that work for me personally. At the moment I have found the best way to look after myself is to do nothing and my nothing can be many different things: learning about how to support the plants that grow in my space, how to be a more present mother and relative, getting a healing from my cat (yes being selfish - not giving but receiving).

The concept of ego versus self-love has been at the forefront of many meditation classes and deeper insights into myself. My understanding of the word selfish has changed. I struggled to understand how can others put themselves first and work, where have I put myself first and acted selfishly without realising it.

I use this method quite often when something triggering happens to me (by triggering I mean something that makes me angry, furious or stuck without seeing options). A recent example would be a conversation with my son where everything I was saying to him was actually what I should have been telling and doing myself. I feel that people who teach us our biggest lessons love us the most. It's a different concept of love that we are used to hearing, seeing or perceiving.

I find it rawer and more basic even almost invisible. It's the commitment, time, energy and effort that another person gives or withholds from us, that allowed us to move to a different space that enables us either to grow and expand or if that growth is not in our best interest then to go inward and contract. It is usually with time we gain perspective, but with an abundance of meditation techniques and self-development tools available I believe all it requires is just a change of intention and focus and allowance of space and pause for perspective.

I find it easy to see situations from the perspectives of different people/participants. I can also see the situation from further away - as they say, take a step back and have a look at the situation from afar, and possibly it's also a good idea to see it from above. I find the trick is then not to lose sight of what is right for you.

Love can be allowing people to learn their lessons by respecting their journey, letting them know at the same time that if they do need help you are there for them. If something is not feeling right to me in my heart, mind, gut I now ask myself what would it take for me to regain my balance?

A lot of time I tried to live up to my family's expectations. Eventually, I saw that by doing that I have actually insured I would not, and I lost all sight of who I was. It took some time and quite a bit of work to find my backbone and my feet. At this point, I recognise people's expectations around me but choose not to be guided or influenced by them.

By that same approximation, I am careful not to have expectations of others. It's not that I don't have them, I still do but I have the knowledge and awareness of this, and I believe this helps me make better-informed decisions. I am happy when I can be helpful to someone. However, like other things this happiness of mine is conditional. It works only when I feel it's on my terms. We all have our own terms. Discovering mine helped me to set the level of what is to expect in life. Otherwise, how would the universe know what to send your way?

Choose you. Be love, life and compassion.

Find beauty in any situation. Whatever happens, ask yourself - where is love in this situation? What is the lesson I am not seeing? What can be done to change this in a way that would suit you?

There are always other options. Sometimes our tunnel vision

stops us from seeing the possibilities and options that we have. The joy of life can be the smallest simplest thing but sometimes it takes working on gratitude and appreciation to fully understand and see what can be right in front of us. I have been through a very long list of situations where I felt and strongly believed I did not have a choice.

Now when a feeling like that comes, I take myself out of the usual environment to reassess my position. I go to a place I have not been before and sometimes also possibly with people that are very new to my circle. This helps to see things from new angles, with new energy and vibration.

Recently when I feel very stuck or am aware that I am self-sabotaging myself I use essential oils of myrrh, frankincense or rose to help me elevate my state of mind and emotion. By increasing my vibration, it allows me to feel and act in better ways. In this way I am caring, supporting and loving myself.

I understand that my mind, body and spirit need an occasional pick me up and it's great to have healthy natural options to do that. Another very powerful part of my self-care routine is taking time for myself to re-energise. I work with people on a daily basis, and consultations where you go above and beyond can be taxing.

For healers I believe it's even more important to place emphasis on self-nurturing as we give so much of ourselves to others during sessions. I love being there for people, but I also know you cannot pour from an empty bucket. I am lucky to have found a massage therapist that is ideal for me and when I feel depleted, I make sure I book in and get the care that is needed.

Receiving regular healing sessions myself also is part of my self-care. I now try to avoid situations getting out of hand. When an issue arises, I start working on my internal, to resolve their external manifestations.

We are all-powerful at manifesting. I've had numerous occasions in my life when I have created the most fantastic and unbelievable situations and circumstances. Some of them were like good movies, others like bad horrors. Lessons that I have taken away are, if you like it and it's your cup of tea (as I have seen it's not everyone's) dream boldly and bravely and make sure you do dream. It's when we create beauty, prospects and success in our minds. And power that up with emotion from our hearts, that's when beauty, joy and fulfilment comes.

On the other hand, be aware and careful, knowing full well just how strong a creator you are, of your less useful or self-damaging thoughts or doubts, or playing out worst-case scenarios in our heads. I am not saying do not be realistic or prepared for any eventuality but rather do not give those type of thoughts power over your focus, emotion or energy.

I had a very recent experience where I had one vivid thought of what would it be like if such and such bad scenario played out. Surely in 3 months it came to pass. Two years later I am still dealing with the aftermath of the nightmare I created first in my head.

A friend of my recently joked that I am very good at creating monsters in my life and that I should rather focus my energy on creating other happier things. Of course, I agree with the concept and now focus my thoughts on ideas that fill me with joy without fear. This helped me to have a calmer and more fruitful way of living. I now treat my mind and thought with the gentleness and love it requires.

For mind support, I love my frankincense and copaiba oils in the morning for clarity and great ideas. During the evenings I enjoy Access Bars recordings and binaural beats. This gives my mind and subconscious an added advantage and boost. I am all in favour of nice healthy cheats to help me go further in development and growth in all areas of my life.

There are so many tricks and techniques out there these days to help us that there are literally no excuses not to look after myself. On occasion, I go through periods of time as one of my colleagues referred to as "contraction". It's the wave in my understanding that comes after expansion when you go into yourself after gaining new knowledge and experiences to chew it over.

Your body and psyche need to process all these new details and adjust accordingly. That's why sometimes we need times of rest, not doing anything and even possibly without much thought ... to allow for further room to be made and new ideas and potential to be uncovered.

That's when beautiful ideas can come our way, as we create space for them to appear in. There is so much talk around the subject of decluttering our homes and minds. My personal experience supports this. If I feel stuck or stagnant, without progress or action I use cypress oil by defusing, and also topically on pressure points on my body. I noticed this helps energy flow around and within me, and I get things done easily, especially those that I have been putting off for a long time.

Also, I felt the importance of allowing my body and mind the time to adapt and learn how to be this new me in these new energies, circumstances, and position of elevated vibration.

To me, love is allowing myself and others to be the way we are with healthy boundaries and compassion among other things. It took me years to realise for myself which values I would not negotiate on and what was key to me. It took even longer for me to find my voice to speak up for myself.

The idea of respecting elders was powerfully ingrained into my being. I was also brought up with an idealist world view. So, when the real-life showed its colours in all vividness it was a shock at first followed by deep feelings of betrayal and resentment. I believed that older people are wiser, kinder and more honourable.

Life taught me people at different ages can act all sorts of different ways and that's ok. It's ok to be 65 or 89 and act like an adolescent. At the same time, it's ok to be 14 and act like a 40-year-old. Now when I see people going through situations in life and judgements pop up in my head (as they do on occasion), I catch myself and ask which part of that either resonates with me in any way or if I am refusing to see within myself?

I forgive myself for judging and always ask what is the bigger picture I am not seeing. It's a great method that helps me to be more in a state of gratitude and compassion rather than judgment. Indeed, it's a more loving way of being, in regard to communication and relationships with yourself and others.

I don't have to go far to remind myself of how much I still need to work on. Earlier today I was reminiscing with an old friend about my experience in managing people at work. One of the areas of concern was hygiene at work. It was a lovely constructive conversation up until a point when I remembered a situation that was still festering like a wound. I exploded with a whole series of unfavourable expressions only to immediately realise after how unhealed I was.

I was full of regret and resentment even more so towards myself for tolerating that behaviour, for lack of professional boundaries and better management skills. Another thing I remember vividly, I always did the best I could in those circumstances as I was already up to my neck with responsibilities.

People do the best they can. Yes surely, in theory, we could all do a bit better, try a bit harder, put in the extra-extra hour. However, maybe it's not necessary. What has been a must for me though personally is the acceptance of my own potential and progress. I have learnt to appreciate that pushing too hard to fast can backfire and lead to unwanted and unpredicted results beyond our imagination.

Like I mentioned earlier we are great at manifesting both the 'good ' and the 'very good'. One of my clients said to me once that all of her days were either good or very good. I was amazed and it shifted my world view upside down. No matter how bad I perceived the day or event to be, it was not bad but good. It was just good. And what was good was just super special. I started looking at the events of my life and new days differently. Situations that used to drive me crazy, I chose to make less fuss about.

When I started looking back in time and noticed that no matter how horrible I felt about a situation there was always a solution to it after, even if I did not see it in the moment. Then it made me think that all that worry I was putting myself through in those moments was simply unnecessary. It was almost as if I believed that the more I stress and worry the more worthy I will be of a good outcome.

I would put myself through a whole self-punishment and judgement process. In contrast, I now have faith that God/Universe/Creator has got my back. I am on the right track as long as I can see a step ahead, I do not have to fret and see the whole picture. I enjoy planning my future but I allow it to be better or different from what I envision.

Throughout my life, people have told me that I want too much or my dreams are unrealistic and I should know my place. For me, loving me is knowing my place humbly while at the same time recognising just how lucky I am with the gift and talents that I have. They are a bit all over the place, but they make me into who I am.

In my opinion, if I can do something as a contribution to people around me and I don't, then it's a potential opportunity that has not been taken advantage of. I have recently done a strengths assessment test. I like rediscovering myself. My motto lately has been if I want to learn about people I need to study and understand myself first.

A lot of what I believed about me was shaped by people around me. How about my own thoughts and feelings? Not my family's', friends' or colleagues'. It's a journey and I still do not have all the answers. I am more aware and present in the now and in myself. I love myself more every day. I love my life more every day and the people in it, in my 'imperfect' loving caring compassionate way, I do the best I can do at any given moment in time.

Family love is another kind of special I want to touch on. How love is passed down, taught and how experiences in a family at times, should come with their own how-to manual. The more time goes by the more I feel they are crucial skills that are underrated at times. How to be in different roles within a family?

What are the healthy ways of expressing love, support, understanding and so on? It's all kind of shown to us on the bases of assumption and directives passed down to us by our primary careers, but not really taught. Then we in turn assume rather than truly communicate. Some families are better at it than others, like we all are, in all aspects of life.

So, I had an experience in childhood that shaped quite a bit of my future life without me fully realising it or giving it due credit. I was about six and even then, decided to put my family's needs first and not mine. I kept a secret which if came to light would irreparably, in my opinion, break the family. My way of showing love for everyone was to keep that secret. I was so good at it that at times my conscious self would even forget it ever happened.

Then other situations happened, and I would always keep quiet. So, the pattern perpetuated without me realising. Then it started manifesting outside the family dynamic: in my health, personal and work life. Only fairly recently in the past 3 years, I have started doing serious work on the subjects.

So, having kept the original secret I have deprived everyone else in the family the chance to learn their lessons. Life might have played out in completely different ways. People could have had the opportunity to raise up or not, depending on their personal choice.

Looking back at it now I see that I loved my family in the only way I saw possible back then. If I could turn back the clock - yes, I would have acted differently, but I did not have the knowledge then that I have now. In a way, it all happened just right the way, the way it was supposed to. I have heard the part of me that felt angry, burdened and resentful.

I acknowledged the pain and the what-ifs that came with it. At the end of the day, I had a choice and made a decision that I thought was best. I respect, appreciate and love my decisions and feel the same way about my family now having more insight into our individual roles, and how we obligate each other to act in certain ways. For a while, I have lived in victim energy. 'Poor' me waiting to be hurt, always on the defensive ready to pounce at threats on the horizon.

The amount of energy necessary for that is huge. I even slept in full alert mode. Even in my dreams, I was aware I was dreaming but had an ear on alert to the real world. All this till I realised during one of the meditations that it was my decision alone who I choose to be. If I choose to feel with every cell in me that I have power and choice, and no one can take that away from me.

I can choose to be feminine and gentle and soft without being weak. It also takes practice just like anything else. So, one thing is to come to a realisation, and another to put that knowledge into practice as mentioned earlier. I advise - take time, practice and be forgiving with yourself, and others around you whilst you are at it.

Recently I have come across an article by an author I look up to and respect. It discussed the mundaneness of the author's life and as a result its lack of provocative potential as a PR option. That in a way, her steadily well progressing and balanced life was a hindrance, because it was not scandalous enough. In a different seminar, I heard a stunning woman actively promoting being provocative as an advertising de facto advantage.

I was curious about both points of view. On one hand, what a blessing it is to have a "picture book" perfect life, on the other, few believe in perfection and want to see life's rawness and gore. Gore sells easier than good ethics, neither is right or wrong, there is a place for everything to exist and be expressed. It doesn't have to be a competition.

My face-off with 'competition' was when one of my businesses was in its maturity stages. I would train members of my team, put my heart and soul into it only to see them leave and create their own start-ups. Back then I experienced it as a stab in the back. How could they?

After episode number three I perceived it in a new light. How amazing it is that I can inspire and teach people how to create their own successful businesses that were doing even better than my own. Wow, I started feeling love and joy for them instead of awkward bitterness and regret. I also learnt that thanks to them moving on I had space free up for new people with even greater potential.

To me, this was a step forward with an intention that felt right. I believe that people that teach us the most, love us greatly, as they show us vividly, time and time again what we need to 'work' on so we can evolve in a sense to a better version of ourselves. I am deeply grateful to all the people I have met on my life's path as without them I would be a very different Anna today.

My work has been my "love" teacher also. I was a very soft person back in the day. Now I am tough as nails and it seems some days, I can chew through rocks. One of the side effects of living within victim energy is that it can spread to your creations. So, if I was a victim my business was a victim too, as an extension of myself. I went through the process of treating my business as my child. It was my baby, my creation. I loved it deeply.

Anyone trying to attack it or twist it in any way always felt like a powerful personal attack to me. Believe me when I say it took quite a few meditation sessions to get over that one. When feelings like that creep over me I release with awareness and unconditional love from my field. Again, it's my own choice and what I believe is right for me. Maybe all my business needs is extra care and attention. Tweeting a few items on the agenda and no heartache.

This kind of brings me back to family issues, patterns and influence. To my parents, their business was their other child. It was fulfilling and traumatic for them as they took every bump closely to heart in the same way I did as I followed in their footsteps. Even in terms of personal life, in the given time period, I have followed a pattern set by my grandparents and parents.

So, no surprises here, I have been looking at ways to break this cycle and the patterns which come with it. The big question is how to do it? Many different healing modalities offer different tools for this. As I like to experiment, I try different ways and look to find what works for me. Commitment to informed self-care has been top of the list for me lately.

I went through stages of healthy living from my teenage years but the motivation behind those habits was vanity and false hope, that if I were to become perfect everything else in my life would be that way too. After that came a stage of disenchantment, when I realised no matter how perfect I tried to be no one cared.

Then followed depression. For me now, self-care is a must without compromise, because if I cannot truly love me how can I even try to love others. To me now my body is a gift that I was blessed to receive. I feel it is up to me now how I look after and cherish this precious blessing.

The same principle applies to my mind and spirit. I value and appreciate their sharpness and vitality. Nurturing all my gifts and talents is my expression of love to myself, people around me and the universe. If done with harmony and balance beautiful results will come to fruition.

To strive to be the best version of myself on any given day is how I live. I try my best to treat people around me with compassion, respect and love. This is my own little way of bringing love into the world.

AUTHOR BIO

ANNA TOKOROVA

Anna Tokarova is a persistent London based entrepreneur and holistic wellness consultant.

She has a Sociology and Business Administration educational background as well as a successful business venture running for over 8 years.

Anna is passionate about promoting wellbeing in all aspects of life and is a certified Theta Healing® practitioner and instructor, Reiki Master and Access Bars practitioner. Part of her unique approach is a fusion treatment method involving meditation, essential oils healing properties and massage therapy.

At present, Anna is running Natural wellness classes empowering people to be pro-active with their health options.

Anna has built her beauty and consultancy businesses from scratch and has first hand experience of what it's like to go through all the ups and downs of such an endeavour.

She is of Ukrainian descent and a single mom to a son and a step-daughter who according to her have been her guiding stars and pools of inspiration. Anna chose to be based in Kensington, London as the creative energy in the surrounding area provides a continuous flow for ideas and new concepts that arise in the fast paced time we find ourselves in.

Her moto professionally is "Go above and beyond for my clients" and personally at present "There's always opportunity for growth and development if one is willing".

CONTACT:

EMAIL: atokarova8@gmail.com

LINKEDIN: www.linkedin.com/in/anna-tokarova

WEBSITE: www.letsgetinspired.co.uk

 facebook.com/anna.tokarova1

 instagram.com/777anicka777

3

BRIDGET GARCIA

MELTING THE ICE MAIDEN

I was born on January 22nd 1972, in a small Fenland town in Cambridgeshire. I was raised at Lattersey Hill Farm with my older sister and younger brother.

Life didn't get off to a good start. I was born to parents who were desperate to have a boy to carry on the Farm. Females were not desired.

Being rejected for who I was brought me many personal challenges. I felt surplus to requirement. A reject. Unwanted. I was embarrassed to be me.

It was a harsh, cold environment to grow up in. There was a distinct lack of love and affection.

Writing my story has been more challenging than I imagined. I found it hard to be authentic, to be honest. Perhaps because I grew up in a home where nobody spoke the truth or expressed how they felt.

I was told it took my Dad 18 months to even look at me. Although married and living with my Dad my mother was in a relationship with another man for many years. He was a friend of my Dad's and sadly he was ever present during my childhood. He would join us on holiday and for Christmas dinner...It was just the way it was and as children we had to accept it.

Farming has been in our family for at least 3 generations and my experience has been that it is very much a man's world. The only expectation of me that I ever heard was to marry a rich man! The men were the bread winners and the women tended to the home and children. This sounds very old fashioned now, but this is the world I grew up in. The inequality between the sexes in some farming communities is clear to see and to this day it still causes much hurt and resentment within my family.

I spent much of my early years feeling like the oddball, the one that didn't belong. I always felt different to the rest of my family.

My confidence was shattered. I felt ashamed, unworthy and undeserving to be (t)here...I use these words now but at the time I just felt like there was something wrong with me, but I didn't know what. This later proved to be a catalyst for me to be as loving and accepting as possible to my own son.

This creation dominated my life for many years and I never wanted to experience this kind of rejection again. I would terminate every relationship I ever got into so that I didn't have to feel the pain again...even the good ones! I couldn't put myself in a position where it could potentially happen again.

When I was 20 years old my mother very casually told me that I wasn't wanted and having felt something wasn't right all my life it almost felt like a relief to finally hear her say these words.

Secondary school was hard because I was so uncomfortable in my own skin. I didn't want to be seen - It was a painful time for me. I went through a period of binge eating attempting to fill the void which only made my self-hatred worse.

Soon after finishing school I was keen to leave England. After my A levels I set off with a friend Inter railing around Europe. This was the start of my love for travelling. In my early 20's I spent time working and travelling in Australia and New Zealand. I had some amazing experiences including working on the Great Barrier Reef and I formed friendships that would later change the course of my life.

With time and space away from my home and family, it was in Australia that I started to read self -help books, anything and everything I could lay my hands on. The first book I remember reading was called "Living in the light" by Shakti Gawain. This book gave me hope. I was finally reading about a way of life that I hoped existed and a life that I wanted to experience.

On my return home from Australia I felt the need "to give back". I went into service, caring for those in need and less fortunate than myself. I worked with children with challenging behaviour and young adults with Autism and learning disabilities. I worked in personal care, as a Teaching assistant and also volunteered helping disadvantaged families. I have always been attracted to the underdog, maybe because there is a part of me that has always felt like one.

This was grounding work...

After several years of mostly being in England I was ready for another adventure. I searched through the many possibilities of where to work and volunteer abroad, and eventually chose to work with Orphans in San Jose, Costa Rica. This trip later took me out to the coast in Playa Hermosa to work on a Turtle Conservation Project where I would meet my husband and father of my son. The marriage was short lived but to this day we remain friends.

I was in my early 30's when I had my son, but I wasn't in a good place. I didn't really know who I was or what I wanted to do with my life.

Now seen as both a blessing and a curse I was hit by postnatal depression. It felt like a switch turned in my brain as I lay in the hospital bed with my newborn son. Undiagnosed for 7 months it was a hellish time. I was disconnected and lonely with no purpose or goal. I was gripped by anxiety and although I was extremely tired, I just couldn't sleep. Through sheer exhaustion one night I hallucinated which terrified and disturbed me. I wasn't coping with life. It was the dark night of my soul.

Life couldn't get any worse.

By the Grace of God my good friend Kerry who I had met in New Zealand had recently been introduced to Avatar - a self-empowerment course that had started to change her life. At the lowest ebb of my life she invited me to attend an upcoming course in Orlando, Florida. Thank the lord, my life was about to change for the better!

The loving care and attention shown on my first Avatar course was second to none. I spent 9 days using the experiential tools of Avatar with trained facilitators and it altered my life forever. The course taught me how to live deliberately and to discreate the beliefs that were no longer serving me. It also gave me some tools to create what I preferred. It taught me to be Source of my life and take responsibility for all of my creations.

The problem was, I had been operating from my mind, believing its thoughts and false beliefs. I had been believing what others thought of me. I didn't know that I could decide and choose for myself. I had been in a whirlpool of mental chaos and absolutely affected by the negativity around me. It was time to take charge of my life and I now had the tools to do it.

Most importantly, I had to start feeling in order to heal. During the exercises in which I was learning to feel again I remember spending several days wandering around the course room doing anything but feeling...my resistance was initially very strong!

However, I was finally starting to see the light. I was a vast and eternal being who had been totally trapped in her own mind.

It was around this time that I started running. I was releasing trapped energy in my body and it made the world of difference. I have never experienced depression since.

I continued on the Avatar Path attending all the courses available. I liked this new me. This happier me was emerging as I expelled more and more false beliefs. I wanted more of it. 15 years later I still regularly use the tools. I have a network of like-minded souls that I work with and they support me to keep growing and moving forward. The tools enable me to stay awake, centered and in control of my life. The blame game has gone, and I am free!

After I had taken the Avatar Master Course (which enabled me to deliver the course) I was inspired to work with others in a Therapeutic role. By this time, I had separated from my husband, left Costa Rica and returned to England with my 1 year old son. I trained as a Humanistic Counsellor in Stamford, Lincolnshire while working in various care jobs.

Once I had qualified, I moved to Kent with my son and worked as a Counsellor, privately and for the NHS. I worked at Kent Counsellors for several years working with hundreds of clients. I worked with anxiety, depression, bereavement and PTSD to name but a few. I loved my job and I will always be grateful for the experience. I have treasured memories of some of the beautiful clients I was fortunate enough to work with.

Self-love and care did not come easy to me. I was highly skilled in self sabotage!

If you are not shown love, then how do you know what it is?

Over the years I have been very harsh on myself both physically and mentally. I burned myself out at work with compassion fatigue and hurt my body exercising. I have had to learn to be kind to myself from the thoughts that I allow to ruminate in my mind to the people I allow in my space.

Yoga helped me listen to my body. When I first started practicing it was all about strength, how far I could push myself, how much I could do. I pushed myself so hard it resulted in a neck injury. I have had to learn to support myself more gently.

Practicing loving kindness is a life -long process. However, when I woke up to my Worth it became easier - I no longer had anything to prove.

It was in Kent that I met the lovely Tina. I would go to her for a reading in Margate when I was experiencing a loss or confusion and I always felt lifted and inspired by her positive energy. I then did 3 courses of Theta Healing with Tina and the girls which increased my intuition and faith in myself.

So along with my Counselling tools, Avatar tools and Theta tools I was in pretty good shape but still there is always more. I came across The Choose Again Organisation online many years ago. They are based in Vancouver, Canada but they have a retreat Centre in Costa Rica.

With my son's father living there, I knew that one day I would attend as I would regularly take my son to visit his Dad. Fast-forward 10 years and in March 2018 I found myself in Paradise on a week long Retreat overlooking Lake Arenal.

The healing process that is done there is based on 'A Course in Miracles'. It takes us beyond the egoic mind with all of its mistaken beliefs about ourselves and others, to the truth of who we all are... it helped me to feel my inherent worth and the love that I am. I later spent a month volunteering on this most beautiful retreat which includes healing processes, silence, gratitude and holotropic breathwork and yoga.

It was on my last day here that I realised that I had been looking for love OUTSIDE of myself...I had been trying to get love from others - my mum, my boyfriend's etc. I finally understood that love is who I am, it is not something I get from outside of myself. Wow!! My whole body relaxed.

The searching, the questing, the striving was over. I had all that I needed. I was complete. I just never knew it!

Happiness is indeed an inside job and 2 days later I met the love of my life! I am grateful every day that this beautiful man came into my life. He is a gift and shows me the true meaning of unconditional love.

Since then I have moved to Costa Rica. My father died suddenly, and it gave me the push to make the move. Life is short and we never know how much time we have left! Life is to be lived now, not in the future.

I have done a lot of work on myself and I'm now enjoying the benefits of it...

I understand that this is just a story. I created it in order to help me grow and see the truth. Without the lessons I wouldn't be the person I am today.

Ram Dass states this perfectly

> "Within the spiritual journey you understand that suffering becomes something that has been given to you to show you where your mind is still stuck. It's a vehicle to help you go to work. That's why it's called Grace".

I love my family dearly for what they taught me, and I feel blessed in many ways ...

I end with the following by the Creator of Avatar:

> "Love is an expression of the willingness to create space in which something is allowed to change"

H.Palmer.

AUTHOR BIO

BRIDGET GARCIA

Bridget is a Mental Health Counsellor, Personal Development Coach and trained Yoga teacher who is passionate about personal growth and the process of becoming one's best Self.

She recently relocated to Playa Hermosa on the Pacific coast of Costa Rica in central America.

She is the mother of a teenage son and lives with her partner and street dog Paulo.

Whilst still settling into her new life she has started to hold self awareness workshops (Avatar) and introduce the Choose again 6 step healing process, a powerful healing modality that reminds us who we really are!

A seeker of the truth since a teenager, Bridget has spent the last 15 years doing her own inner work and being in service to others.

She strongly feels that we can only take our clients as far as we have gone, therefore we must continue to do the work if we want to achieve maximum benefit for others.

Looking back over her life, she can see that her journey has really been about Love, clearing the way for an open heart that was closed for too many years.

The path to her awakening has not always been easy. However, it has brought her more peace and joy now than she ever thought possible.

"Our task is to learn, to become God-like through knowledge"

Brian L Weiss, MD.

Feel free to contact her at : bridgetgarcia@hotmail.co.uk

4

DEBBIE STURGE

hey say what doesn't kill you makes you stronger and I've come to believe this is true! When faced with challenges over the years people have often told me what a strong person I am, although there's been many a time I haven't felt it, or indeed wanted to be.

Like when I lost my dad, a dear aunt and then my younger brother in the space of fourteen short months. And now, facing the reality of a mum with vascular dementia, who slips away a little more each day and barely acknowledges me. But if anything, this has taught me that life is for living and you have to enjoy every moment.

I've not always been a positive, upbeat person, far from it. My natural default was as a glass half empty kind of a girl. I anticipated worse case scenarios, expected people to let me down and blamed everyone else when something went wrong. But, at the same time empathy has always been one of my strengths and I am a good listener.

I genuinely care about people. I am an introvert and shyness has held me back at times, but I'm always there for others. This hasn't always served me well and I am choosier now about who I hang out with. I've come to realise you can't help people who aren't willing to help themselves and I'm a little less tolerant than I used to be.

Over the years I've had way more than my share of self-doubt, limiting beliefs, fear of failure (and success), and for a long time I felt like I was treading water, unclear of my direction in life and what I 'should' be doing. In my gut I believed I was destined to fulfil a larger purpose, but just what it was I had absolutely no idea. I now know the importance of working on myself daily.

Even now it would be all too easy to fall back in the trap of homing in on all the things I haven't yet done, but I choose instead to focus on my amazing achievements to date, like reaching my black belt (2nd Dan) in karate in my late 40's! I am a work in progress, but I'm no longer scared to follow my dreams and I love the fact that this inspires others to take steps towards their own goals. I am a completely different person to who I used to be. This is my journey.

I've always lived by the coast, in Thanet, despite my dad coming from Manchester and my mum from Essex. I grew up with two brothers (one older, one younger), in a strict Victorian style family, where showing affection was not the done thing. I used to be quite envious of anyone who naturally oozed warmth and passion, but if I was approached with a hug and a kiss it left me feeling awkward and uncomfortable.

I'm not saying I didn't grow up in a good, solid family environment and I probably had a privileged upbringing. But only a few years back I was asked straight out if I'd ever felt really loved and I hesitated. I was very close to my dad, he was the best, but my relationship with my mum was a lot more complex. I always felt the need to seek her approval, to constantly achieve in order to prove I was worthy of her love. But no matter what I did, it just never felt enough.

Was I spiritual as a child? Not really, more curious and I can clearly remember getting into trouble at school for using a Ouija board! Mum was a practising Christian and dad 'found God' much later, but I struggled with the notion you had to sit in a stuffy old church every week in order to be a 'good' person. And the more my logical brain developed, the more I struggled. As a teenager, I rebelled against it all.

I've always accepted there being a higher power. Throughout my life I've said prayers and given thanks, but I was probably in my 20's before I really started to explore spirituality. I found it fascinating. What I didn't realise was that God was just another term for Spirit, the Universe, Source energy, call it what you will, but they definitely resonated better with me. Nevertheless, as far as my spiritual journey was concerned, I was still just dipping my toes in the water.

I met my husband when I was just 16 years old. We got engaged on my 17th birthday, were married two and a half years later and I had our daughter just before my 21st birthday. Life was pretty good, for a while. Unfortunately, I didn't take to motherhood quite as I'd imagined and following the birth of my son three years later, I suffered post-natal depression. It wasn't diagnosed for well over a year, at which point I felt like I was completely losing the plot.

It was a pretty desperate and lonely time. I didn't feel like I could admit to anyone I wasn't coping, especially not to my mum. She'd been quite vocal about me being far too young to start a family, just as she'd been negative about me getting engaged and then married. Although she needn't have worried. My husband and I will be celebrating our 33rd wedding anniversary this year and I love him more than ever!

But getting back to this low point in my life, apart from the fact I wasn't coping well as a mother, or a wife come to that, I felt I'd completely lost my own identity. I felt worthless, to the point I was convinced no one would miss me if I was gone. I even resented my tirelessly hardworking husband for going off to work and 'escaping' to some normality everyday, a resentment that festered and resulted in a short separation at one point.

I was resentful of anyone who, as far as I was concerned still had a life, while I was stuck at home with the kids. And then I felt guilty about that. I did after all have two amazing children who I loved more than life itself. How could I think like this? My logical brain was totally screwed!

It finally hit me that something may actually be wrong with me after I headed out to get the car tax one day. A pretty straightforward task and certainly not one you'd expect to have a complete meltdown over, but that was what happened.

After taking forever to kick my butt into gear, get my baby son and toddler daughter dressed and ready to go, and then trek all the way down to the Post Office only to find I'd got the wrong documents with me, it was the straw that broke the camel's back. I broke down and sobbed hysterically, angry and frustrated that I had become so useless.

On the plus side it woke me up to the fact I needed help. Aside from the necessary trip to the doctors, followed by a visit to a hypnotherapist, when I decided anti-depressants were not the way I wanted to go, I knew I needed to put something else in place for me. I was no good to my family in the state I was in.

I didn't realise until many years later that what happened next was a clear demonstration of the Law of Attraction at work. I didn't even know such a thing existed. But I do remember a conversation with my sister in law about how I wished I could find something of my own, that would give me a sense of purpose. I also joked that if, in the process, I could please have to go away on my own for a weekend every now and again, that'd be the icing on the cake!

What manifested was a three year nutritional therapy course. I had always been very passionate about healthy eating and so this seemed perfect. When I found out the course was held in

London and would mean me staying up for a weekend once a month through the academic year, I was beyond excited! I won't deny I wasn't scared to death and even the thought of travelling to London by myself was almost more than I could bear, but it was exactly what I needed. And aside from a qualification for a new career, it gave me that sense of purpose again.

It was a tough three years but worth every minute and I graduated with distinction from the Institute for Optimum Nutrition (I.O.N.) in September 1999. This is another thing I should just mention. It didn't matter what I did, simply scraping by was not an option.

I was so hard on myself and always set the bar ridiculously high. Again, this likely stemmed back to my belief it would make mum happy and proud of me, but it certainly hadn't made me popular at school. In fact, I was extremely unpopular at times, and very unhappy and confused.

On the one hand I wanted to do well to please mum and dad, but equally I desperately wanted to be liked and fit in. Sadly, in my experience, the two didn't go together. And to make matters worse, when I achieved good grades, I was then denied from following the career path I'd set my heart on but told instead I was destined for sixth form and University. Not that this panned out, after a rebellious summer that year. So, it was an especially proud moment when I graduated from I.O.N., albeit some years later, to become a Nutritional Therapist. I started practising straight away.

Having spent my 20's bringing up my two children, I focused on my new career in my 30's. I loved advising people on their diet and the satisfaction of helping them overcome health issues was priceless. For the first time in my life I thought I'd finally found what I'd been searching for and the thing I was destined to do forever. I felt happy and fulfilled, for a while.

But being a therapist was tough, especially in the area where I lived and during the grip of a recession. I ventured further afield and practised from the Institute's clinic in Putney, London, and also from clinics in the villages of Headcorn and Hythe. I was even licensed to practise on the beautiful island of Jersey for a while, but it meant spending too much time away from my young family. Much as I craved a successful career, it would not be at their expense.

I was then offered a position as a second year tutor for I.O.N. Although I initially doubted my ability to do it, as was typical of me, I was becoming more familiar with stepping outside my comfort zone and knew the challenge would do me good. I've always believed things happen for a reason and this was an opportunity I couldn't turn down.

And I'm so glad I didn't, as I absolutely loved it. It made me realise another passion, to help others develop and grow. It was such a joy and so rewarding to coach and inspire them towards their own success, and I felt honoured to play a small part in their respective journeys. I've been drawn to teaching roles ever since.

After three years I reluctantly gave up tutoring for ION, but structural changes had made the role difficult to manage. I was also going through a very challenging time with my daughter, now a teenager, and our constant battle of wills left me an emotional wreck. I was desperate for support, but it wasn't forthcoming. Once again, I found myself spiralling downward and just as before, I really believed everyone would be better off without me. And the guilt I carried, that I'd failed as a mother, was unbearable.

It was a difficult time to get through, being all too easy to focus on the things I believed I'd failed at, of which there were far too many in my opinion. My self-worth was completely down the toilet. But I knew this couldn't be my lot in life. I knew, deep down, I deserved better. I started reading books like 'You Can Heal Your Life' by Louise Hay, 'The Journey' by Brandon Bays and The Celestine Prophecy, in an attempt to find some answers.

Gradually I picked myself up and shifted my focus back on work. I was offered an office job at my local Age Concern centre and decided to give it a go, alongside my nutrition practice. I loved working as a therapist, but also found it lonely and isolating at times. I craved company. However, what was initially a very straight forward and basic admin role, evolved into a hugely stressful management position, with a threat of redundancy hanging over the centre.

I worked like I'd never worked before, and would often work in the middle of the night when I couldn't sleep due to the pressure. I felt responsible for everyone else's job and for the people who visited and relied on the centre. I was still juggling my nutrition practice and alternative, healthy weight loss groups, and I was at breaking point.

At the same time, I became a Nanna for the first time! My daughter moved back home after two years living away and presented me with a grandson. It should have been such a perfect time. I was overjoyed with the birth of my gorgeous grandson, but because of all the stress I was under I didn't have the time, or the energy to enjoy him, or help my daughter. I was exhausted mentally and emotionally and became irritable and snappy. Those all too familiar feelings of guilt and not being good enough started to surface again.

Just before Christmas 2011 I met with social services and felt a huge sense of pride to be told that our centre had been the most improved in the area. But it turned out I'd only won the battle and not the war. About a week later we received news they were shutting us down anyway and we were made redundant three months after. All the work and stress had been in vain and I felt I'd failed everyone. To make matters worse, I ended up in a row with my daughter who then moved out with her partner and my tiny grandson.

I was in pieces. I didn't know which way to turn and was totally burnt out. I couldn't seem to do anything right. I knew I had to take a step back and seriously work on myself again. I started reading about transcendental meditation (TM), booked myself on a course to learn it and was soon meditating twice a day. It wasn't a quick fix, but it definitely helped me cope better with stress.

I felt ready to return to work and took on another office manager role. I told myself that this one would be different; especially given I'd be working from home for the most part. But it wasn't. The more I did and proved my capabilities, the more I was given to do - the workload was ridiculous! But it didn't matter how hard I worked; I simply couldn't keep my head above water. I felt as though I was on a hamster wheel, trapped and with no way off.

In an attempt to deal with some of my challenges (or more likely block them out), I started full contact, knockdown karate! Having just turned 40 it was met with a mixed response, but I'm not sure anyone really took me seriously and midlife crisis was mentioned. But I wasn't going to let anyone put me off. I trained hard, built up my strength mentally and physically, and gradually worked my way through the grades.

After five years I was ready to take my black belt, but with doubts creeping in I had to work just as hard on my self-belief in the lead up to my grading. I harnessed the powers of visualisation, affirmations and EFT. Every night before I went to bed, I would thank the Universe and visualise in detail being presented with my black belt.

It was nonetheless a gruelling, six hour grading and definitely one of the toughest things I'd ever done, but I did it! I was beyond proud and it still remains as one of my greatest personal achievements ever, despite going on to take my 2nd Dan two years later.

Around this time, I was approached to teach a karate class and felt really honoured, but once again self-doubt took hold. I wasn't the most experienced black belt in the class for one and I didn't think I could do it, but after speaking to a couple of close friends who laughed at the very idea of me turning it down, I agreed. A very different teaching role, but the experience was amazing.

Meanwhile I was totally disillusioned with my office roles and craved to return to my therapist roots but wasn't convinced nutrition was the answer. In the early days I'd believed everyone could achieve optimum health and essentially be cured with the right diet. I liked the fact that nutritional therapy was science backed, and black and white.

But I began to realise there was something missing and that correct nutrition, while important, was not the be all and end all. Through my years of treating numerous clients, not to mention my own personal journey, I've realised nutrition is only a piece of the puzzle. If a person doesn't have the right mindset, or energetic vibration, optimal health will still likely elude them. The mind, body, spirit connection simply cannot be ignored.

So began my spiritual journey on a more serious scale. I met Tina Pavlou initially when she came to me for nutritional advice and I was totally in awe of her energy and the amazing, spiritual things she spoke of. She had become known as The Angel Lady and her vibrant energy was infectious. I attended several of her workshops, thirsty to learn more and then together we went to an Abraham Hicks, Law of Attraction event in London.

I knew Tina also taught Usui Reiki and was intrigued to know what this healing system was all about. It's not something I'd have had time for as a newly qualified, closed minded nutritionist all those years earlier, but my mind was much more open now. Having said that I'd shown no interest to learn Reiki and was surprised when Tina announced to me one day that she'd booked me on her next course to learn Level 1. But then it's said that Reiki finds you and in my case, this was definitely true.

This was early in 2014, just as my 87 year old dad was scheduled to have heart surgery up at St Thomas' hospital in London. I had planned to stay up there so that I could visit him with mum, and I remember it being an extremely tough, emotional week. Not only due to dad's serious surgery given his age, but also because it was pretty evident (although not formally diagnosed at this point), that mum was showing signs of early stage dementia. Looking after her while navigating around London to visit dad was far from easy.

The Reiki course was booked for the day after my return from London and I can remember wishing I'd not agreed to it, as I was mentally exhausted. It was the last thing I wanted to do, or so I thought. But it couldn't have been better timing. Not only was the day so restful, positive and uplifting and exactly what I needed, but I was attuned to beautiful Reiki energy. I became a regular at Tina's reiki shares and psychic development classes. I loved the energy, the positivity and the beautiful souls I was sharing my time with. And I was able to put Reiki to good use straight away, to help my dear dad.

While he recovered well from his actual heart surgery, dad deteriorated in other ways. He soon struggled to get about and developed an agonising pain in his arm that would have him cry out, and dad was not one to make a fuss. I was apprehensive offering him Reiki initially as I didn't know how he'd react, but not only did he agree, he went on to have almost daily treatments over the next few months.

It was absolutely incredible to see how it helped relieve his pain. Had I in anyway still been sceptical, this proved to me beyond any doubt the power of this gentle healing system, and I was so grateful to have been attuned to it.

I went on to take my Level 2 and am convinced Reiki helped me cope in many ways during this time. Not only the obvious, being able to help ease dad's pain while benefiting from healing at the same time, but emotionally too. I'll never forget our special time together. But while dad continued to deteriorate, mum was intolerable and particularly during a time when they lived with me.

They were not managing dad's morphine correctly, but with him away with the fairies as a result and mum not comprehending what was wrong because of the dementia, it was a nightmare. I was desperate to help them both. I took over dad's medication and continued his regular Reiki sessions, but this made me extremely unpopular with mum.

I don't know how I held it together, but knew I had to remain strong for dad. He was appalled by mum's behaviour towards me, but I think she simply couldn't cope with the reality of losing her husband of 53 years and I was an easy target. I have no doubt the dementia played a part, but it didn't make it any easier.

I was heartbroken when I lost my dad in July 2014. It was nothing to do with his heart in the end, but cancer niggling away in the background. Ironically his heart was the last thing to give out. I continued to give him Reiki when I could, even in the hospice. I knew in the short term it would help relax him, but ultimately, I believed it would ease his transition.

The effects of the morphine, his ongoing pain and the evidence of his struggle as he so desperately didn't want to give up and leave us, was more than I could bear. Much as I didn't want it, it was a blessing when he finally passed.

Mum wouldn't allow me to have any part in the funeral arrangements, nor would she let me choose my flowers when she sorted out hers. My younger brother was living in America at the time but had managed to get back just before dad died and was the only one mum really turned to. It didn't surprise me or my elder brother, as he'd always been her favourite. There was nothing we could do.

For a while I felt lost. I knew I'd done everything I could for dad, and this gave me some peace, but at the same time I now faced the huge responsibility of looking after mum. It didn't help that we'd always had such a difficult relationship, but her dementia was making things worse. But she was still my mum and I couldn't bear seeing her so lonely, and I was worried that she wasn't looking after herself properly.

I offered for her to live with me, but she declined. I tried getting help for her, she blocked it. I visited everyday to make sure she'd taken her medication correctly and had a meal ready for the day, and she despised me checking in.

I couldn't face doing Reiki and stopped meditating, two of the things that could have helped the most. And as if I was on self-destruct, I took on a third office management position. I don't know why I thought things would be different, when I kept on repeating the exact same patterns. I don't know why I was surprised when I found myself heading for burnout for the third time in succession. But I knew I needed to take a long, hard look in the mirror and be totally honest with myself.

It was pretty clear that the common denominator each time was me. I had 'allowed' each of the situations to unfold, and then reacted badly when they had, and I'd felt trapped and backed into a corner. I realised I had to learn to say no when necessary, to resist the temptation to be a perfectionist, and to ask for help (and equally importantly, accept it), when the going got tough. And I absolutely needed to take back my power, raise my vibration and practise forgiveness!

I started offering Reiki again. A friend came along for a treatment and knowing how unhappy I'd been, suggested I should take a look at network marketing. I was extremely sceptical and not at all sure it sounded like an ethical business, but knew I had to make some serious changes so agreed to take a look and was blown away.

Not only did I see a way to return to health and wellness where my true passion was, but the entirely flexible business would fit easily around my family commitments and down time. It was June 2015 and I couldn't wait to get started.

I was motivated again and excited. I was sure I'd finally found my true calling and knew I'd be able to work my new business around my nutrition and Reiki. I was helping people with an amazing range of natural health products and fulfilling my passion to teach as I mentored others in the business. I learned the importance of mindset and ongoing personal development.

I ignored the negative people around me who said it couldn't be done and it wasn't a proper job and worked hard. I set goals, created a dream board and smashed my first promotion in just six weeks. I was on fire and proud of it! And then, just as everything was going so well, I received a phone call in the middle of the night with devastating news.

I couldn't even make out the voice at the end of the line initially and I nearly hung up, thinking it was a prank call. But then I heard the words that will haunt me forever. 'He's dead. Dave's dead' Dave was my baby brother.

I felt sick. I couldn't believe it, nor did I want to. Dave had been hit by a car and killed instantly. He was only 46 years old and had four young children. I never imagined a day when I'd have to travel to America to arrange my brothers funeral. The last time I'd seen him was at dad's funeral just fourteen month earlier.

Dave and I had been really close as kids, but he'd lived abroad most of his adult life and we'd drifted apart. But worse than that, we'd had some major disagreements since dad's health had started to deteriorate, as I felt he should have made more of an effort to visit. Dave was not the easiest person to get along with, very much taking after mum and could be very intimidating at times. But he was still my baby brother.

When I returned from America, I threw myself into my new business, more so than anything else I was doing. I craved the distraction, but he was always on my mind. I doubt I'll ever get over losing him. It really highlighted how fragile and delicate life is and that we absolutely must make the most of it.

I never take anything for granted now. I practice gratitude, meditate and work on my mindset daily, I am always reading inspirational and spiritual books, and am constantly learning. Knowing what a difference it has made to me, I am extremely passionate about inspiring others to follow their dreams, to believe anything is possible with the right mindset and action, and to help them become the best version of themselves.

I've come to understand just how complex life is and that the journey is rarely straight forward. Even the most spiritual people have many challenges to overcome. Contrast is there for a reason, there is no dark without light, and we can't appreciate the great stuff if we don't experience challenges.

It has taken years of personal and spiritual development, and mindset work to reach where I am now, but I'm still learning, growing and evolving. I believe we all are. Life is after all a journey, not a destination! I believe we must embrace and always be grateful for what we have, take full responsibility for where we are and understand we absolutely are masters (or Goddess's) of our own destiny.

In 2018 I became a Usui Reiki Master Practitioner and have already begun teaching. I'm still practising nutrition and continue to grow my network marketing business and am always looking for enthusiastic, likeminded people to join me, who have a genuine desire to help others.

I am a certified Law of Attraction Life Coach, have just completed my Angelic Reiki levels 1 and 2 with Tina, and am starting my Theta healing journey with her in September 2019. And I am writing my own book.

Whatever your dreams are in life I encourage you to set long-term goals, but then break them down so you don't become over-whelmed, disillusioned and give up. When I started karate, I didn't think about becoming a black belt, but trained hard to get my first red belt and then my second. Love life and it will love you back. But most of all, be prepared to leave your comfort zone, as this is where the adventures happen!

AUTHOR BIO

DEBBIE STURGE

Debbie lives in the seaside town of Margate with her husband Paul and dog Harley, has two grown children and three grandsons she adores. With a background in Nutritional Therapy and Reiki, and a black belt in Karate, it's since starting a network marketing business in 2015 that Debbie has become especially passionate about inspiring others to follow their dreams, to believe anything is possible with the right mindset and action, and to help them become the best version of themselves.

After graduating as a nutritional therapist in 1999, Debbie practised in London and from various clinics in Kent, and on the island of Jersey. She was also a tutor for the Institute for Optimum Nutrition in London for three years.

Learning Usui Reiki Levels 1 and 2 in 2014 with Tina Pavlou, Debbie delayed taking Level 3 after losing her Dad, but became extremely passionate about the healing modality after witnessing how much it helped him. Focusing initially on self healing and developing her own spirituality, Debbie went on to become a Master Practitioner / Teacher in April 2018 and is now teaching. She has also been attuned to Angelic Reiki.

Fulfilling a lifetime ambition, Debbie took up full contact karate at age 40 and achieved her black belt five years later. She taught her own class for a year and achieved her 2nd Dan two years later.

Alongside being a therapist Debbie worked in office management for several years, but it came at a cost. After reaching burnout for the third time in succession she realised she was not living her true purpose and was being guided by the Universe to work through important lessons. Taking a leap of faith, she started a new business in network marketing, working alongside a global health and wellness company.

Although previously sceptical she is now a strong advocate of the industry, believing it enables 'ordinary' people the opportunity to live extraordinary lives. Having been drawn to teaching / mentoring roles over the years, she gets tremendous satisfaction helping others develop and grow, and is looking to mentor others in her business.

Debbie has studied EFT and NLP, is a certified Law of Attraction Life Coach and is currently writing a personal development book. You can follow her on her dedicated Facebook page 'Debbie Sturge, Inspiring Change', for regular tips on health, nutrition and exercise, mindset and personal development.

As she continues her own personal development and spiritual journey, Debbie's mission is to inspire others along the way and help them find their true purpose. She firmly believes a fulfilled and abundant life hinges on good health, a positive mindset and great energetic vibration - total harmony of body, mind and spirt - hence covering all aspects in her work. And you'll often hear her saying, 'life is for living'!

For more information, or to work with Debbie, please contact her via:

info@foreverbodywise.co.uk

http://foreverbodywise.myforever.biz/debbie/

 facebook.com/changewithdebbie

5

DEBBRA SCHEMBRI

*H*ello beautiful soul...Do you feel a restlessness or a deep yearning for something more?

Do you feel the call to change your life but are unsure how to do it ? Do you feel the call of the Goddess, the call of your soul ?

Maybe like me, you've been through your awakening and have already made significant life changes, and yet you feel the call to something more, to enter into another phase or maybe you're just beginning on your growth journey.

Either way I hope that what I share here speaks to you in some way so that we can share part of our journey together.

The goddess is reawakening in us all, the unconditional love of the divine mother.

Humanity is now in the process of experiencing a major energetic shift as the universal balance of power begins to realign. Hallelujah!

The time of operating from the dominant, driving, masculine (god) energy is coming to an end. This transition is paving the way for a cosmic union of the god and goddess energies; the yin and the yang, the active and the receptive, the dark and the light, the seen and the hidden, the science and the mystery.

This era brings feminine energy back into its rightful place alongside the masculine. The king and the queen united as one force.

The God and Goddess energies working together create a powerful force of transformation, taking action to resolve some tough problems we have, with love, and the much needed elevation of our consciousness here on earth.

This touches us all on a very personal level in the balance and connection between our head and our hearts, our thinking and our emotions, our own masculine and feminine energies within.

How do I know? Because this balancing act has touched my life in a profound way and been a significant part of my personal healing and transformational journey, as well as a part of my souls purpose and life's mission.

I began working in the consciousness and healing field in the early 90's way back when it was a very different landscape. I was teaching meditation, manifesting, emotional intelligence, energy healing and all manner of modalities and methods that are common now, and not considered way out anymore but rather are very popular.

Back in those early days I was called a witch or cult leader at times, feared or joked about, but I was on a very strong soul directed mission, and I never let that stop me.

I did thousands of private sessions, channelled soul guidance readings but for personal development not predictive work. Reading the causes behind any life problems or health issues and then clearing and resolving them using various methods, way too many to mention. I also did spiritual and soul development and a whole lot of learning and teaching.

I became very well known for my accuracy and had a busy healing and training centre and a big community that I called "Synergy of Light"

I created an 18 month holistic healers training programme and also trained teachers to share this body of work. I ran many and various courses, transformational retreats and overseas spiritual journeys. I took groups through Peru and the Amazon and ran my first of countless spiritual journeys in Bali, back in that time when it was a more unusual thing to do.

These days I still work as a soul intuitive, healer, success coach, transformational teacher, retreat leader and mentor to conscious business people and light workers. Those on a mission already or those who want to change their lives and live a more soul directed life. These days I enjoy the freedom of being able to move around and spend half of my time in Bali and the other half teaching internationally.

I love that we can now easily have a global reach not like those early days. I have co-founded a charity and a turtle conservation farm in Bali and do all kinds of community service work there as well as run cultural and spiritual healing retreats and Tors. I work with the balancing of the god and goddess energies as we need both.

So that's been my life's work since my awakening nearly 3 decades ago now, however I had a whole life before then.

There are so many things I would love to share with you however I had to pick just one thread from my life story, a very challenging task !

The title of this book is "When the goddess calls", I am honoured to be involved and I used this theme to inspire my choice of what part of my journey I could share.

I'm sharing my pre-awakening time. When the goddess called me loudly to wake me up. Some of my challenges and ups and downs in the wish that it inspires or speaks to you somehow.

Before my spiritual awakening, I was caught in the great dream we call 'life'. Often, in times of crisis my soul would give me messages, but I wasn't ready to listen to my guidance back then.

I moved from child to teenager to young mum, fumbling around in the dark. The lights were on, but nobody was home. With hindsight I call this phase the 'walking wounded'.

It seems that as humans it's often our journey to learn about love through experiencing what love is not.

I always was aware of being different, having a secret inner world, but I can honestly say I wasn't conscious of what it meant. I now know so many of you feel the same way.

The goddess is calling more and more people now. She's calling us to remember her, to remember why we are here. She's calling on us to wake up and to wake up others.

She called on me back then, and calls on me now to keep going, and evolving, keep checking in with my own inner balance of these energies.

I would like to share a dream I had back in that time that feels now like a past life it was so long ago.

I was in a temple with a lot of other people milling around. There was a large impressive statue of a goddess. Slowly the statue started to move and come to life and to break free of its concrete base.

Everyone was screaming and running, myself included, but I was at the back running more slowly, scared but at the same time fascinated, looking back over my shoulder at her.

Why am I scared, why am I running? I wondered. I stopped and turned around to face her and woke up out of the dream.

This prophetic and symbolic dream was showing me the changes I needed to make personally; namely to stop running in fear and instead turn inward to meet the supernatural empowering goddess force within me, to wake up out of my dream, my life, my unconsciousness. The energy was wriggling and moving inside of me and I kept shoving it down and getting on with life, as we do. What energy was running me? More importantly what was I running from?

At that time, I was doing the usual things trying to be what I thought was a good person.

Letting go of control and listening to my heart and intuition, the voice of my soul, was such a big challenge and I was running scared of whatever this was, rocking my boat from within.

I had created a good life for myself according to what we're told we should want to make us happy.

The god energy, the masculine power pushes, strives, achieves, controls, and gives form and structure to things. It is the fire, the mental level, the mind, logic, reason and action. It doesn't want to stop and listen to feelings and it certainly doesn't want to get lost or stuck relying on wishy washy intuition. This yang part of us usually feels very uncomfortable with vulnerability, with showing the underbelly, as it sees this as a threat to its very survival.

The fear is that if we make ourselves vulnerable someone will use it against us, and sad but true that can be correct. There is a feeling of needing to protect ourselves, and our masculine side is the protector within.

We do need this masculine god force; men and women also, we need the yang because it keeps us safe, it protects and provides, it can make clear decisions without getting overwhelmed by emotions.

This god energy is not the problem, instead it's the over valuing of it coupled with the demeaning and undervaluing of the goddess; the confusion, fear and denial around the yin aspect of life and the problems that this imbalance creates that we need to rectify. We've been living in a patriarchal world for so long that we have accepted it, it's become the norm, but ancient history tells us that it hasn't always been this way.

Before my reawakening I was completely out of balance in myself. I looked feminine, walking and talking like a woman, but I was being driven by a very yang energy. I believed this was normal, it was the way to survive, to be loved and valued and even to be successful. Now, I maintain that success and even our survival as a species rests with us balancing out these energies.

We need to bring forth that nurturer, the carer, the healing energy. With the feminine, goddess, great mother energy we look after others, we care for ourselves, we take time to be, we see the whole picture and are not just focussed on one part of life. We use our intuition, our empathy and our emotions. We listen to our feelings and our silent knowing. We cry we dance we sing we create.

Humanity has a bit of a mess to clean up now. We need these energies to come into harmony and balance, to be courageous enough to shine the light on the parts we're ashamed of or don't know how to handle so that we can become whole again. This is vulnerability; this is a part of the goddess force. The one who gives birth to new ways, more peace, this is the divine feminine.

One key thing I have learnt on my journey that I would love to share with you is that our challenges, wounds and lessons are personal yet not. It is a great paradox.

Yes, they are personal, our experiences are real, and we all have a unique story, however the same challenges are collective, it is a much much bigger story than just us as individuals.

As a collective, as a humanity, a race of beings, we are growing through and evolving through certain lessons, and changes to evolve as a species. This doesn't make it easier to know this however when we realise that we are a part of this evolution of consciousness it can take the pressure off the negative feelings we can burden ourselves with.

The self-judgement, the blame, guilt or shame, the separateness we can feel. We are all in this together growing through what we need to grow through to become more of who we are. More loving, wiser, more accepting, more balanced, more compassion-ate. More empathic and caring and connected with each other.

I remember the time when my mission and life's work was new for me. My inner world was rocking, and my soul started to speak to me rather loudly. The booming voice I call it. The whispers I'd been hearing most of my life increased in volume and I could no long suppress the messages coming through. Back then I had no clear idea of what I'd come here to do.

The words life purpose, mission, soul journey, life's work, passion, all of these things were never in my mind. What was in my mind was the ordinary thinking of how I could create a good life, be a good mum, provide for my family, have a nice house, and not struggle. I was brought up very yang, surrounded by loads of active, entrepreneurial energy. The make it happen, push, strive, work hard, create, get on with it, be powerful, be strong, don't be weak, emotional, soft, masculine god force method of being successful.

Like so many others at that time, intimate and vulnerable communication was not present, emotional connection was minimal and there was always a lot of 'busyness' and activity.

I look back now and find it fascinating that I had no spiritual people around me growing up, no books, or triggers in that sense that would lead to my soul awakening.

It definitely came from within, emerging from the depths of my being like a natural energy demanding to be expressed, like that goddess statue in my dream coming to life, cracking me out of my trance.

I remember the feeling I had then, It felt like I was holding back the tide and I was so tired inside, not physically tired but a deep soul feeling of tiredness.

I surrendered within and let go of the struggle of holding this feeling that I couldn't name. This was the moment I let the goddess energy into the mix.

I had a fear that I would lose control, and everything would come flying out, and this is what happened. I even had this secret fear that if I let go, I might go mad, that I wouldn't be able to handle it, even though I didn't know what "it" was. My ex-husband admitted to me many years later that he did fear that he might have to take me to a mental hospital as my psychic abilities surfaced. I also feared that if I was vulnerable and transparent with people around me that they wouldn't love me or want me anymore. I felt a lot of shame, guilt and fear of being open and honest and exposing my inner secret world.

This fear tracks back to some traumatic experiences that began when I was 3 yrs old and being told that if I told anyone what was happening, that no-one would love me or want me anymore. That fear burnt into my little mind as an absolute truth. It became what we call a bottom line belief.

At about 4 years old I did try to open up to the person who was looking after me at the time. I was screamed at, shamed, called terrible names that I didn't understand at the time, and was accused of lying and rejected. It proved what I had been told, I wouldn't be loved or wanted anymore.

Consequently, I hid things and created secret places inside myself - this is what we call the shadow. My shadow became dark and heavy. I split off little parts of me, incidents that I couldn't integrate. I blocked things out and carried on as normal, smiling, putting on the happy face, the mask, because that's what we do... right?

I just wanted to be normal like everyone else. Throughout my life I knew that I was hiding things that I was ashamed of, but I thought that was the way to handle life, to be strong, move on and not let things that happened to you ruin your life. Well there is truth in that, but what I didn't know then is that there is nowhere to run and nowhere to hide.

Everywhere we go and, in every moment, these unresolved events, negative and critical thoughts or feelings about ourselves will plague us, festering beneath the surface and sabotaging all the beautiful things that we create. They may appear by disturbing our sleep, or affecting our health, our relationships, or our success. Sometimes, they feed addictive behaviours or encourage a lack of self-care or make us feel numb or depressed or anxious or out of control emotionally. Tragically for some even suicide.

Some of this happened in my teenage years, when I was living on the wild side trying to numb myself with addictive behaviour, taking too many risks and not caring for myself in many ways. I was rushed into hospital at 18 in severe pain and they took out my gallbladder. There was nothing wrong with my gallbladder but there was plenty of blocked toxic emotion and inner pain going on and it was starting to manifest physically.

This was the first time I am aware of, that my soul spoke to me and said...

"Debbra, this is the first body part you have lost, and they will just keep cutting things out. You know what this is about. You need to stop and look within".

I wasn't ready to do that then; I considered it but didn't know what to do, so I just kept going on my messy path. The next time my soul spoke I was 20. I was living the work and party lifestyle at the time. At a party one night I got very drunk, fell over and hit my head. I was knocked unconscious for a while and when I woke up, I headed home not in good shape. The next day after a long and heavy sleep I woke up with a sore and bloody head, suffering a hangover. This time it said...

"Debbra do you want to live, or do you want to die? If you want to die, then keep going because this is where this path leads. It is serious now you need to choose".

This time I made my choice; I used my yang energy to pick myself up, push everything down again, get control of my destructive and addictive reactions and head home to start on a new path. A much better choice, but the problem was I still hadn't dealt with anything. I was still the walking wounded.

There was no one to talk to and I didn't know how to deal with my situation so I just used my strength and will power to control myself, put my mask of being okay firmly back on and continued on with my life. That's what we are taught to do isn't it?

All of my life I have been on a mission. As a teenager I was on a mission driven by my inner critic and my wounding. My critic was fuelled by guilt and shame. This came from events that were actually nothing to do with me and were in fact totally out of my control. I truly was a victim (OMG! I said the V word!)

Sometimes we really are victims, but that doesn't mean we have to let those events define us. It doesn't mean that we have to live our life as victims. At that time, I didn't understand that though. In my teen years I was living like a victim, angry at the world for what had happened to me, overwhelmed and confused by the emotional wounding and hidden baggage I carried.

The 'me too' movement has revealed how common these experiences are, and certainly as a healer I have been both privileged and saddened to assist hundreds heal these wounds and many others. The fact that I survived those teen years really was a miracle.

After my teenage years I was on another mission; to get myself the things that I had been taught would make me happy. It was a programme that was running my life! I thought it was me, yet it wasn't. In alignment with the programme, it didn't take long before I met a country boy, fell in love, got married and had a family. I was very driven to get ahead in life, make money, be self-employed, own property and follow in the footsteps of my business orientated family.

It was a very yang way of living, and as I said, I looked like a woman and acted like one; I was affectionate and cuddly; I loved to cook and loved my home, but my energy inside was very unbalanced. Despite the fact that I was in my mid 20's, I had a wonderful life, a loving husband, 2 amazing sons, a successful business, a house on the beachfront, a rental property - I was like a ticking time bomb waiting to go off.

When I look back now, I can see that my marriage, my beautiful family and the successful life that I was actively creating, really had no hope of surviving, not when I had all of these negative thoughts, feelings and beliefs about myself, that I was just pushing deeper and deeper down. My spiritual self was always there, but I never stopped to have a good look at it. It was like being two people, the self of my secret inner world and the masked self that was busy crafting my life.

The desire to keep running, working, achieving was strong but I couldn't run away from the truth, that I had never stopped to go within and meet myself. At this point I still hadn't had any counselling or spoken to anyone, about anything. There was no resolution, no release, I was just holding everything down and controlling everything that had previously exploded as a teen, but that I now had 'under control'.

I knew something big and intangible was missing, and I felt guilty about that feeling because my life was pretty good. I felt like I wasn't being authentic, but I didn't really understand why.

In my field of work, I have come across many successful people who aren't happy. I have also discovered that not everyone has had a wounding in their past. I have met many who have lived blessed lives and been given every opportunity, but who have struggled a lot with their own inner relationship or with specific aspects of their life journey.

Some have grown up in a perfect family but may have a perfectionistic streak which can block them from creating. Some have been given every possible support but feel obligated or expected to become a high achiever; they feel they have to constantly strive, and they burn out because nothing is ever good enough.

There are many common issues that people struggle with like the inner critic for example regardless of whether they have experienced trauma. None of us learn how to deal with our own thoughts or emotions. Something so basic, that we all really need, and yet don't get taught. What I am trying to make clear is if you haven't had wounding or traumas it doesn't mean that you won't have challenges. They come to us all.

When they come, if we don't have the knowledge of how to deal with them, instead of just pushing through them, we end up experiencing some kind of consequence. We can shut off, become too tough, strong, or hard, without even realising it, or we can numb ourselves in any manner of ways. That's how we lose ourselves and get overwhelmed.

I now feel that absolutely everything that has happened to me makes perfect sense.

My personal belief about this is that I chose it all. I chose this life, the year, the era I would be born into; I volunteered to come and work on bringing more awareness, and love and to do my tiny little bit in the evolution of human consciousness. I carefully chose all of the particular wounds and experiences that would shape me into the person who needed to heal herself. I have no blame or ill feelings towards anyone.

My path was to be a healer and a teacher of soul, higher consciousness, love and awareness, holistic success and happiness. I came specifically to be a light worker, in service to the goddess energy through educating others on emotions and intuition, and through guiding people to love, to find inner peace, and to create amazing things.

I opened myself to channelling through spirit, healing energy, messages, and divine guidance. I merged business and spirituality by being a nurturer and supporter, a mentor and guide to others on their path of personal transformation and changing our world.

Growing up I never would have imagined such a life path; I wasn't aware of any of this back then. I went through the Catholic Church education system so God, Jesus, the Holy Spirit and Mother Mary were more familiar to me as a spiritual path.

As a child I was very drawn to the church, which I now realise was my strong spiritual side. I used to see a smoky kind of purple light that looked like a thick fog; I decided it must be the Holy Spirit and it made me feel safe. As a teenager I learnt about other religions and I felt like I had woken up out of a dream. I felt a little tricked.

I was a bit angry and disillusioned with the church and that was when I stopped going. I did have some psychic experiences as a child and teenager, but I suppressed them all. I don't remember crying much as a child - I do remember a nun when I was in primary school screaming 'don't cry, don't cry', at me because I had tears rolling down my cheeks in class and I don't think I cried again for another 10 years or more.

This caused me to create what I now know as the well of unshed tears. I was emotionally blocked, and I had mental blocks from suppressing memories and splitting off little pieces of myself that I felt were not okay.

Some people are overly emotional, which is a common lack of balance, many are shut down; mine was the yang way, disconnected and numbed to my emotions, being strong.

During that awakening time of my life I could feel an unconscious programme running to split up my family and re-create the drama of a divorce; what had happened to me as a child. I had enough self-awareness to recognise it, and to see the patterns that wanted to play out. I tried controlling it, but the energy was stronger than me; it was after all my karma, my life lessons.

I describe it as like being on a train, knowing it was going to crash. I knew it was going to create a lot of damage, but I wasn't able to stop it or get off that track. So, when the next soul intervention came, I had been married 7 years and we had created a lot.

"Debbra you need to take more time and go for walks, spend some time alone reflecting on your life. You are recreating your childhood that didn't work for you - it didn't make you happy then and isn't making you happy now".

As the messages were coming, they were unsettling me and making me question my life focus. There was a restlessness stirring inside of me. I started going to bed early after putting the boys to bed. I'd light a candle and spend time alone. On one of these nights I had my first mirror vision. From where I was sitting on the bed, I could see the dresser mirror in the distance. I saw very clearly a fortune teller with a crystal ball and a man standing by her side, they looked straight at me as I looked at them.

Unseen energies seemed to be flowing between us and what was coming to me was that I was seeing myself in a past life or another dimension. The message I received was that it was important that I was not to work as a predictive psychic in this life. It really surprised me, and so at that stage I told no one.

I started going to bed and meditating and even though I didn't really know how to, it just happened naturally. I started taking some time off work and taking long walks on deserted beaches. I was trying to follow my guidance and sort out my inner world alone, as I always had.

I had no guide to help me make sense of what I was experiencing. I became more distant from my husband as I felt myself changing from within. Then my experiences started to ramp up. I went through an awakening, and although that makes it sound gentle like waking up from a dream, mine was more like an explosion.

At this point the lid well and truly blew off Pandora's Box. My husband and I had a general store and post office and when people came into the shop, I could hear their thoughts and feel their feelings. I knew how they felt about themselves, their bodies, their relationships. I could see behind the masks and the thin veils.

I started to feel myself merging and blending with people, so that I literally became them. I could feel their features, their hair, everything. It was as if I was looking out of their eyes. It scared and confused me because I seemed to have no control over it.

Telepathy, empathy, clairvoyance, clairaudience, soul blending, all of these abilities were surfacing. My healing energy was switching on although I didn't know then, that's what it was. The palms of my hands were heating up and pulsating. I could see auras around people and see life force energy. I was hearing the booming voice once again, but this time it was constant and becoming louder and louder.

"This is a nice life Debbra, but this is not the life for you. You are a healer.

You need to heal yourself and others. You need to be learning and teaching.

You are here to help others wake up. If you just help one person, that would be enough, but you are here to help many. You are here to work with consciousness.

If you do not change your life and be your true self, you will probably get cancer and die".

That was a very scary message. I didn't know what a healer was. I knew what a naturopath was, I had felt drawn to that in my past but I had just pushed that aside but a healer, no consciously I didn't really know that term but something inside me knew for sure and I made my choice to surrender to my soul purpose. It was a very confusing and messy time; my marriage didn't make it and I dis-mantled the life that I had worked so hard to build as I changed all of my priorities and my drive changed.

I now know that I could have had it all, my soul purpose, my real mission and all of the good things I had created back then, including my marriage, but at that time I didn't have the tools and knowledge, clarity or maturity to hold it all together as I went through such a dramatic shift within which changed my whole life focus.

Are we driven by and lost in our mission, even our sole purpose? I see that a lot. Women who are sacrificing everything else because they think it's the most important thing like I did. I had to learn how to be clear and resolved, to feel and release, to understand and integrate, to forgive and let go of the toxic energy in my emotional body.

To handle the suppressed old memories that were surfacing. In those days it wasn't as acceptable as it is now and there wasn't much help available, so it felt like getting a machete and having to cut a path through a jungle. Hard work - so I could heal myself bring myself back into balance, embrace my divine feminine within and then be that guide for others, someone who has walked the path before and knows the way.

One of the things I've been able to do in my work has been to help many couples through their rough patches and I feel proud of that, it's very rewarding work for me as I know if my husband and I had really good guidance we probably would have navigated my changes differently.

I had to figure out how to use these gifts, for some reason it was important that I wasn't a clairvoyant who did readings, rather using my abilities as a psychic healer, personal growth counsellor helping others with their transformation, holistic success and happiness. I had to figure out how to start feeling and integrating the divine feminine into my life. I had to become vulnerable, wow, that one was a biggie. I had to roll up my sleeves and do a lot of self-exploration.

I had to learn to control my abilities, so they didn't render me unable to function in the real world and that was a challenge for sure. I had to learn that emotion is energy and you cannot control that energy by blocking and suppressing it without severe consequences.

Another key thing I have learnt that I would like to share with you is this.

Emotional energy needs to flow, and it needs an out. That out could be talking therapy, writing, singing, dancing, breathing, sounding, various techniques but there needs to be a release, resolution and an expression. To heal something, you need to let it go. You may need to process it in different ways first, but you must let it go or it will never shift.

Negative thinking needs to be controlled; the monkey mind needs to be mastered.

I started practicing diligently and teaching meditation, healing, manifesting, with many and various methods and systems for personal transformation, very quickly. Once I surrendered over and changed my life and started seriously working on myself the teacher and healer in me just birthed, already experienced and confident, very driven and on a mission to help as many people as crossed my path.

In the later 90's I was meditating in my healing centre when I first received another clear message

Debbra you need to take a group to Bali on a spiritual journey

Bali? I questioned I knew nothing of the spiritual side of Bali, only that it was a Touristy place but yes, the message was clear. I put out the call to my community and quickly got 20 people to join me on my first overseas course. I went to a small village on the west coast as I had been drawn to it, and I still take groups to that same village to this day in fact this is where I am right now writing this. At the turtle conservation farm, we are a healing and teaching centre, also with a homestay.

Many people run retreats in Bali these days but back all those years ago it was not so common. I never could have imagined then that I have a deep soul connection to Bali and the Balinese people. I have had many experiences here, highs and lows and have led countless groups here over the years. My journeys and offerings have evolved greatly here over the years as I deepen my connection with the culture and my experience grows.

I could write a whole book on my magical experiences in Bali, but I will share only one with you as it was very special and had a big impact on me.

I got to a point in my journey where I had helped literally a few thousand people. Not with a high profile, not by being famous, but just by working and being committed and very focussed on my path. That is one of the changes I don't love in my field, so many wanting to be famous and all the marketing hype stuff but that's another story.

I got to a time when I had this restless feeling again, I felt as though my mission was done, I was feeling a yearning for home and I mean the spiritual home. I didn't want to leave my boys, they were now grown up, but they are the one thing that really keeps me here (still), but I was missing something badly the restlessness was strong again.

I was feeling so clear, light, sensitive and open psychically. I was having spontaneous and detailed past life recalls that were visual, emotional and energetic. I could remember my past lives and was consciously working with my karmic themes. I was also having these energy downloads and activations.

When I had these experiences, I would ask someone to sit with my body because when I felt it coming, I knew I would be out if it and I needed someone to hold space for me. I had also been seeing light beings around me for many years, they were always around when I was teaching or seeing a client and they are still a part of my life now.

This one time I had just finished running a spiritual journey in Bali, it was around the time of the September 11th twin towers bombing. I felt the feeling coming on, one of the ladies in my group had chosen to stay on a little longer after the retreat so I asked her if she could hold space for me and watch my body.

I lay down on the floor. My body starting vibrating at a very high and fast rate. My solar plexus seemed to be the source of this energy and it built and built until I felt like I would explode into light. I know now that this is the area in the body where the incarnational star sits. You may have heard of spontaneous combustion. I felt like I was about to explode into light.

All I could feel was this incredible love, I felt so fulfilled in this love, like I never needed anything again, I was complete, I was home. 4 light beings appeared to me in my mind and started communicating with me and this is what they said ;

"Debbra we know how you feel. We know that you feel you have completed your mission but you still have more to do. Feel this love, this is your true essence, this is the truth of everyone.
As you can see you cannot be this truth, this LOVE, and function there where you are so all you can do is hold as much of this love as you can. Ground it and bring it into the physical so that you can share it with others and they can benefit from this energy. We know you feel alone but you are never alone, we are always with you."

They reminded me that I had volunteered to come, that it was my choice to incarnate with this mission of working with love and higher awareness, wanting to help with the shift of balancing the masculine and feminine energy once again.

The goddess returning to earth. They reminded me it was my role to support the upcoming healers, light workers and change makers. They then guided me through my birth, being in the little baby body and how powerless I felt at that time, being so vulnerable and dependant on the adults around me.

They took me through some of the experiences that I had as a child where people had abused my vulnerability and misused their power over me. They took me through some other lives and showed me this had been a theme. It seemed to be around the masculine energy, power issues, abuse issues, the imbalance of power between the male and female. Sexual confusion seemed to feature as well as spiritual misuse of power.

In all the lives they showed me I had been in the spiritual, religious or healing world somehow and there was abuse of power in there also. It was clear that there was a reason I had avoided being involved in any particular religion or even spiritual or healing system this life.

I have never been into the guru thing and always aware of giving away power or it being so important to empower others also and help them to be independent not dependant on me or a system for their power or growth. It was an amazing supernatural experience and I was left feeling so pure, incredibly cleansed and almost unable to speak for a few days, rendered speechless in awe of the divine love energy.

I was just quiet and still riding in this incredible enlightened reborn pure feeling. They knew what I had been missing, craving, that Divine Love, that connection and sense of meaning, I needed that experience and needed a reminder of why I am here.

The message was this that yes, I had helped enough people and I didn't HAVE to do anymore. My mission in a way was complete but now more than ever my mission was to support and hold space for other change makers and light workers.

It was up to me how I wanted to proceed, but that my mission was now to hold this love energy. They told me that I was to create a retreat centre somewhere where I could be the space holder and create a place of love and higher awareness. They said It didn't matter where the retreat was. I was also told I had work to do in Bali, helping the people there.

So, after that I continued on with my retreats, guiding people and doing spiritual work but also started working with entrepreneurs and conscious business owners. You see for me light workers are not just the spiritual folk.

Light workers are active and still awakening, literally everywhere because we need them everywhere. So many conscious business owners and entrepreneurs now merge money and spirituality and we have change makers in every profession in the mainstream, all making the world a better place with their contributions.

Everyone can be a part of the solution by living their best life, being loving and kind and awake and aware of the impact they have on the world and others. Working together side by side as we redeem ourselves and re-create this reality. We make space for the feminine goddess energy, the divine mother unconditional love energy and integrate it into every system and every area of life.

So now my mission now is simple, to hold a space of love as best as I can at all times and use my natural abilities to connect to soul level and this divine love to help people fast track on their own journey. To guide others to higher awareness and unconditional love. To be happy healthy and successful living their soul directed life, like myself.

I am so grateful to have been around long enough in the field to see the fruits of our labour manifesting. We have Reiki in some hospitals, schools and aged care facilities, we have mindfulness and personal development in corporations, and mental health is getting lots of focus. We have work/life/balance movement and a strong and thriving complimentary medicine field.

We have heart centred business people and ethical investment opportunities. We have many issues being flushed out seen and addressed. We have high profile people like Oprah promoting healing, self-work, and all manner of great stuff and we have Marianne Williamson running for president of the United States, amazing, I never could have imagined that back then when I first began!

The goddess is returning although she never left. Let's all slow down, stop running and turn to greet her.. welcome her into our hearts and our homes. We really can have it all, the best of the divine masculine and feminine working together, the yin and the yang in harmony and balance.

The love and connection of family, children and relationships as well as our life's work and mission. Not sacrificing ourselves and helping others to the detriment of our loved ones, something we nurturers and care givers need to watch out for, the dreaded martyrdom. We don't need to suffer.

I would love to meet you one day. I wish you well, so much love and happiness to you and thank you for joining me for this little journey. I would love to connect if you feel you would like to. Let's all hold the vision of the world we want.

And create together a healthy world of balance, and loving awareness.

Thank you - I love you -

Debbra Schembri

Australia/Bali

AUTHOR BIO

DEBBRA SCHEMBRI

Debbra Schembri is an Australian energy intuitive. A gifted and compassionate guide, teacher and healer with a natural ability to connect with your soul.

She believes that when we meet heart to heart, soul to soul, and hold a safe and sacred space magical changes occur.

She works intuitively with groups and individuals to channel higher awareness and has many skills to help you on your path of empowerment.

She specialises in helping her clients to find greater clarity and see the bigger picture. How the specific challenges they face are an opportunity to grow. This brings a deeper meaning and a clearer connection with their soul. She helps her clients to manifest the life they want, the love, success and happiness in any area of life by co-creating with their soul, and step by step becoming their highest selves, living their life purpose.

She began working in Australia in 1992 after a soul wake up which changed her life from the usual material focus to a spiritual focus.

She especially loves to support other healers, light workers and change makers, including the conscious business people and entrepreneurs, as a soul based holistic success coach and transformational retreat leader. Her grounded nature and earth mother energy brings a practical element to her spiritual work and she loves to support the empaths and sensitives of the world.

Debbra has nearly 30yrs experience as a facilitator of change. For individuals world-wide she offers her one on one coaching and guidance programmes over the phone (or Skype) and transformational retreats in Bali and Adelaide. No two programmes are the same as they are designed for the individual person and their specific needs and desired outcomes.

For groups she runs Connect2Soul designer retreats and trainings with various themes in Bali and Australia. She also teaches internationally when invited and loves to collaborate and co create with other facilitators. She runs healing training and helps other healers fine tune and hone their skills.

She has been running spiritual holiday adventures in Bali for over 20yrs and has a deep soul connection with the land and its people.

She offers immersions into the Balinese culture, spirituality and magical world of energy healing. She loves to do sacred women's work, deep sexual healing and awakening, and is a passionate believer in the need to balance the yin and yang energies for success, health and happiness.

Debbra is a totally mushy grandmother and feels blessed to have two awesome grown up sons and their families, one in Bali and one in Adelaide. She loves the diversity and adventure of living in both places. She is a free spirit, a modern-day mystic, a world traveller who loves to meet new friends and old around the world. She loves the sun and the beach, nature and the simple moments laughing at the craziness of this life.

Her greatest dream would be to see holistic self-education taught in schools. She believes we need the knowledge of how to manage our own thoughts, feelings, stress, and sexuality taught alongside reading, writing and arithmetic.

Debbra is passionate about giving back and community service. She is a founding member of a charity in Bali that restores dignity to the million or more Balinese people living below the poverty line without basics like a toilet.

This part of the real Bali is generally unknown to the many Tourists that visit and enjoy the island and its gifts. She is also a founding member of the Bali Turtle Conservation Farm, a project working to build the numbers of sea turtles and loves to share the joy these beautiful creatures bring with visitors to the farm.

Debbra would love to connect with you or if you are interested in her work you can schedule a free discovery call.

By email on debbraschembri@hotmail.com

Facebook messenger   Debbra Schembri

By text on +61407807610 Australian mobile number or Whats app

Join the Facebook group Connect2Soul with

Debbra Websites www.debbra.com.au www.healerbali.com

6

DONNA-MARIE MILLER

My first very clear memory of my life journey was when I around 5 years old. I can distinctly remember the old avocado green bathroom suite, brushing my teeth getting ready for school. This memory is so vivid I can actually remember the touch as if it was yesterday. Whilst brushing my teeth I clearly felt a soft but a firm two taps on my shoulder. I turned around straight away thinking it was my mum telling me to hurry up, but to my surprise there was no one there.

There were only my parents in the house, and I thought they were playing a game, but I ran downstairs, and they were sitting in the living room. When I told them, I remember them smiling, giving me some excuses about the wind or my hair touching my shoulders, but I knew exactly what I felt, and it definitely was none of the reasons my parents gave me. This was never spoken about again and I just put it to the back of my head and I never thought about it after that until many later years.

I never experienced anything similar until years later; I would say I was about 11 years old when I started to see pictures, which felt like looking at dreams. However, these pictures would become real. I would tell my mum and she used to just smile, probably thought I was going through a phase until I clearly saw my mum dropping me off at our local shop and mum drove just down the road and her car was driven into by a red car.

I could see the day, the weather the colour of the car that hit my mum. I told my mum straight away as I was scared and concerned this may happen, again I was given the look of is she crazy, and just reassured this wouldn't happen. A couple of days later my mum dropped me off at the shops and my mum went and turned the car as I had seen previously, and she was hit by the red car exactly as I said. I think my mum then started to realise this was not something I could make up.

This incident scared me, and it also scared my mum, I could tell from her reaction. From this I manged to ignore the thoughts and what I saw, It was almost like I had put those thoughts in a drawer as I didn't fully understand them, and they made me different from everyone else. This is not what I wanted whilst going through puberty when your body is changing, I didn't want to stand out or be different. I was already very tall and I didn't need anything else to make me stand out.

I was always curious growing up, I couldn't decide what or where

I wanted to go. I knew I wanted to leave education as soon as I could as I found it quite simply boring. I picked up teachers were not particularly bothered, and nothing really captured my attention other than PE and art, I didn't particularly enjoy school. I can recall a careers advisor (I think that's what they were called) asked me to complete a questionnaire to see what I may find interesting as a future job.

My results came back as a receptionist or a hairdresser. I was confused as I showed no interest in any of the options. My response from the careers advisor was this is what your personality is guiding you towards. I can recall thinking what a joke, but the best part from the questionnaire was we were supposed to look for work experience in these lines of work.

I knew I didn't want to do either as I had no interest in these career paths so I took it upon myself to find something I may be interested in. Luckily my dad worked within a large company in Croydon and asked on my behalf if I was able to complete my two weeks work experience there, which they agreed.

I remember sitting in my dad's car nervous, dressed very smart on my first day and my dad telling me to work hard and who knows I could get a job at the end of it. I worked so hard I loved the freedom, people speaking to each other, smiling, I loved it and they told me if I did well in my GCSEs to get in contact when I finished school.

As soon as I got my GCSEs, when my other friends were going to 6th form and college I managed to land a job, working at my work experience placement. I absolutely loved it; however, I didn't love the 4 hours a day travelling, and it took its toll and I left this job after several years.

I started to work at a travel agent in Dover and the difference was noticeable. I remember feeling stuck and bored resting my head on rattling old train window watching the rain bouncing off. The train was dark, and I was thinking Donna what are you doing?

Thereafter every three years I would change my job. I couldn't get settled and I didn't know what I wanted to do, I didn't really know who I was, as a lot of people do. Then out of the blue saw an advert to become a Police Officer, I thought I would give it a go, and got through the interview process and found myself standing in uniform ready to start my adventure of my 2 year training to become a Police officer. I was surprised by how proud I felt in my full Police uniform.

We had to complete a 15 week training programme at a training school in Kent and I remember turning up with my wheelie suit-case, smiley totally naive and innocent to the real world. Walking to what was like a dormitory room, which was very old fashioned. Men and woman separated, mealtimes at certain times.

Marching practise on the parade ground by a shouting drill sergeant. If an officer of ranked walked passed you had to address them by rank and get up if they entered a room, it was totally out of my comfort zone. My room consisted of a bed, window, sink, wardrobe and a desk. Toilet and showers were shared. This took me some time to get used to, this way of living.

After a difficult time at the start due to simply trying to adjust, I ended up absolutely loving it. I made the most amazing group of friends. We supported each other through the training as sometimes it was just hard. We laughed so hard through those 15 weeks and don't get me wrong we also cried, but friends were made for life and I was fortunate enough to share my experience with two wonderful ladies Gemma and Dawn.

Gemma was so organised and definitely the mum of the group who spent so many hours sorting my revision notes into some kind of order and my equally crazy friend Dawn also known as my tattoo sister (something done whilst at training school) who was the best listener and gave the best hugs however the worst at a power nap. (Power nap, not a 12 hour sleep). These ladies certainly helped me get through those 15 weeks.

After I was posted to my area, I soon realised that I was so sensitive to some people because I just wanted to hug them and remove them from the situation they were in, however that was not always the case. This is when I quickly realised, I need to harden up. This I did and when I think back people used to say me, Donna you have changed, which I never understood but now I do. I had to change to get through my everyday life.

I did love my job and realised my passion in the Police was to interview suspects and victims and this is where I concentrated my career. I am proud to say I was a Police officer, and I learnt so much. When I had my own children, my priorities changed. I wanted to be home on bank holidays, I wanted to tuck them into bed every night, so I decided to leave.

Chris and I were truly blessed with our three children, our twin boys Ashton and Ewan and our daughter Maisy. Ashton and Ewan who are such caring, thoughtful boys but totally different in personality. The moment they entered my world my life changed; I had never felt unconditional love like it. My boys are typical teenagers who loves their sports and computer games however football is their passion.

Ashton is an amazing goalkeeper and Ewan is super midfielder/striker. I have spent many a wet, windy and cold morning watching them, and I wouldn't change it for the world, maybe just a few more layers or one of those little tents. I love watching them grow into young men, Chris and I are immensely proud of them and love them both so much.

We were blessed again with our gorgeous daughter Maisy, a mini me. Maisy has the most honest and kind heart, which is a gift on its own. She loves crystals, Reiki, drawing, creating and meditation. Anything I create Maisy is not far behind, my shadow. Maisy has shown a keen interest in Reiki and she is amazing at it. I know she will carry on my journey one day in her own unique way. I love this little magical soul so much.

After leaving the Police, I worked in a secondary school working with children from 11-18 years old. My instruction was to use this space and use my skills to help children stay in class. I knew I could help them, as behaviours must come from somewhere. As soon as the students came into my class to spend the day with me, I would start the day by sitting them down and talking to them but most of all I would listen with no judgement, other than to help them.

This would take the students by surprise and in some cases the children would burst into tears as someone was listening to them. This period of my life I had lots of guidance and self-reflection and I can recall sitting in the classroom thinking why have I been bought here, as it was so different to the Police that I had worked so hard for, I felt a lost again. I knew it was for me to help others and start me on my new path in my life and I was amazed how much I enjoyed delivering a subject and I was good at it.

Over several years I worked in the inclusion centre and listening to the students I was blown away how they felt about themselves, their expectations and pressures of today and how hard it was for them. I started to run courses to help certain students. I then became aware of Mindfulness and meditation.

I studied Mindfulness for a year and passed with a distinction. I am now a fully qualified Mindfulness practitioner for children and adults. I surprised myself as I realised that I did enjoy learning and I was actually good at it; It is amazing what happens when you are interested in something. I would then start to use Mindfulness on the children to help them with their own anxieties.

One of my proudest moments were seeing higher aged students 16 years plus joining me in guided group mediation, and they loved it. The staff didn't, but the students did. I don't think the staff understood, they thought it was an easy way for kids to do nothing, but actually it was the total opposite it had an amazing positive affect.

This gave the students much needed time to calm down or to think with a straight mind. I didn't think sitting a child down with a work sheet looking at a wall would achieve anything other than annoyance and confusion. However, I was made redundant from this role, but I am so appreciative to have worked with amazing students and I wish them all every success as they are truly inspirational individuals who can achieve anything in life.

I noticed as my choices started to change my direction started to change, even simple things down to holidays. I was no longer drawn to the normal holidays I wanted to see the world. I travelled to Marrakesh for the first time with my husband for a short trip away, and wow my senses from the time we landed were alive.

Marrakesh is such a beautiful country, amazing people, fantastic foods and the buildings and the colours, so intense and bright. The first time I walked through the old town Souks, the excitement I felt inside from seeing the amazing colours from the bright red, yellows and orange spices or the bright pinks, greens and blues from the scarves made me feel alive it was simply amazing. Walking into the square and watching the locals laugh sit and talk.

Speaking to wonderful people who were so welcoming, one even offered my husband 12 camels to buy me, he was tempted, of course I am joking. He was a Berber gentleman with the most amazing smile; I truly fell in love Marrakesh.

What I loved about Marrakesh was the unknown it was almost magical. I remembered walking to a restaurant down a dark alley and I was a little apprehensive as it was just me and my husband and a vast difference to the vibrancy I had witnessed so far.

We came to a tiny thick wooden door with black studs over it; we had to duck to get in the doorway, let alone my poor husband who is 6ft 4 he almost had to crawl through it. What we were greeted with a scene which was simply breath taking, opulent chandeliers of candles, amazing artwork, candles everywhere. No roof, just stars gleaming through. I can easily say one of the most beautiful restaurants I have eaten in, and the food, so much flavour, full of spices; I felt a very lucky lady.

We visited a beautiful garden with extraordinary plants, bright and deep blues and white, simply stunning and whilst sitting in a garden café with tiny little birds chirping as they flew past I noticed the most beautiful woman, her skin immaculate and she was wearing a wonderful electric blue scarf covering her head, and wearing a bright deep pink dress, with simple gold jewellery. After that day seeing her embrace these magnificent colours, I decided to bring more colour into my life, with my own clothes and my home and this is where I fell in love with travelling.

My life started to change professionally within my time at the secondary school, through my Mindfulness training, I became grateful, compassionate not allowing my mind to overthink or create. Paths became clearer and I was ready to take steps that I was blinded to beforehand, and this is when I met the amazing Tina, who introduced me and trained me in Reiki.

I came across Reiki from my husband Chris. When I met Chris in a sticky floor nightclub, seeing his beaming smile which lit up the room, I knew this was the man who was going to be in my life forever. 19 years later he is still here, and I have so much to thank him for as he has supported, loved and helped shape the person who I am today. I am a very lucky lady I love this man to the moon and back.

Whilst going out with each other, I would massage him, and I would notice warm patches on his back. I would point to them and he would say that hurts and it became a sort of game. He would have an area that would hurt, and I would find it. I couldn't do anything with it just find it and point and say, "It's hot here".

Then friends and family would come around and it would be, Donna see if you can find where I hurt. This makes me giggle in a way as I had to prove it to others what I could feel, which I totally understand as I wouldn't have believed it until I witnessed it for myself. The Police side factual facts.

Chris was the person that mentioned Reiki to me, he came home from work and said, "I know what you can do with your hands, it's Reiki". I was intrigued and researched it and noticed you needed to be trained by a Reiki Master. I was unsure about this as I had thoughts about a man in a dressing gown, this put me off.

Then I noticed one of my Police colleagues had posted on Facebook stating she had bought her new Reiki bed, and the rest is history this is where I met Tina, who I am pleased to say was not in a dressing gown, I would like to add, just a wonderful talented beautiful lady.

From meeting Tina, I then became part of a strong like-minded group of ladies where I was able to be myself. I started to believe in myself and the pictures that I stuck in a draw started to come alive again. I was able to see and hear again.

I then became a Reiki Master after this I was so keen to keep learning about Reiki as this was a definite gift given to me. Tina told me all about Angelic Reiki 1 and 2 and I was unsure, and I think I was unsure due to the name Angelic. I loved energies but unsure on Angelic, however I told myself to stop overthinking it and see how it goes.

On the first day of my Angelic training I accidentally forgot to set an alarm, however at 7.30am the exact time my alarm would have been set for I was awoken by a continual tapping on my bedroom window. I looked at my alarm and thought I must have forgot to set my alarm and what was this tapping? I opened my bedroom window there was a bird tapping its beak on my window; it looked at me and flew away.

I turned around and me and my husband just laughed, and I remember saying I think I need to go to my course. I can easily say never in the 9 years living in my house has that ever happened and nor has it ever since. During the course Tina had all the angelic cards on the table, they were beautiful cards and I felt very connected. We were going to start a mediation to see if anything came through.

Mine was clear, a beautiful tribal warrior type lady, with amazing hair and warrior type lines under her eyes and a necklace. This was so clear, and I couldn't wait to go up and see if I had come across and Angelic energy. However, nothing matched mine, which made me question yet again if I was right for this course.

The next day I went back, and I asked Tina where she got the cards from as I thought they were beautiful and that I told her I felt a bit sad about my very clear image from my meditation that it didn't match anything on the table and I explained what I had seen.

Then Tina lifted the booklet out of the box of cards and one card fell out, my warrior lady Archangel Ariel, I will never forget it. Both of us couldn't believe it, well Tina could I am sure. After this I completed the course and completed my Angelic Masters. I now use my beautiful Angelic cards all the time, they have guided me so many times and I now use them alongside my Angelic readings. We work perfectly together.

I have got video footage on the day I can home from my course and my dog Rocket is sitting on my bed. I'm calling for angel energies and Rocket simply goes crazy barking at the space next to me, it was amazing. I shared this with the group, animals are great at picking up energies. Love Angelic.

After practicing Reiki several of my clients asked if there was any training as they loved our sessions and what came through, which again was very easy for me when healing. I decided to go ahead and start to teach Usui Reiki and I now have a wonderful Reiki group of amazing individuals who meet every month to practice Reiki and to share experiences.

I love the fact that people are opening their eyes to holistic therapies and become part of a supportive network and I love seeing their lives and perspectives change, just as mine did. For this I cannot thank Tina enough for being there for me, supporting and believing in me.

After I was made redundant, myself and my then colleague who also worked with me decided to help others with our Mindfulness and our police background and DC Breathe was created. The DC stands for Delivering Confidence and the Breathe part is a tool we use to calm the active mind. So far DC Breathe has helped 1000s of people from 1-2-1 work, beautiful one day retreats, corporate training and staff training, working within schools with students, families and the NHS.

DC Breathe delivers corporate training all around the country from Brighton to Birmingham. I feel alive standing on a stage or presenting what I am passionate in, and this feeling comes from working in front of the class. If you can deliver to a class of grumpy 14-year olds you can deliver to anyone. Some of these courses we were not even allowed to give the course a name, as people wouldn't come and discuss Emotional wellbeing.

I remember standing in front of 15 men and about 3 woman and

I explained what the day would involve and why we were there. I have never seen so many awkward men, their energies, body language was fully shouting, HELP !!! After I explained don't worry, we didn't turn up in a van full of incense and we wouldn't make them chant, they calmed down and that course was one of the best.

I'm good at gauging an audience and adapting to that audience, this is one of the amazing skills I gained from the Police. You had to adapt all the time to deal with whatever was in front of you, and I have been able to carry this forward with me.

Seeing the difference in this group from the beginning and at the end seeing the same group starting to open up, talk and share experiences and the fact that somehow, I got them all to meditate for 15 minutes at the end. The response was outstanding. We received so many emails after that course thanking us.

I have worked with so many clients on a 1-2-1 basis using Mindfulness and Reiki. Working alongside extremely anxious individuals. Anxiety, stress can be so debilitating and the fact I can help and watch my clients enter their first session at their lowest point and leave after several sessions, watching their personal journey to the point they are leaving a totally different person, it's one of the best parts of my work. It absolutely fills my heart with joy.

I have completed some really amazing work with families, as I feel this it is so important for the whole family to understand. I also feel and hear that families get left out. One person in the family unit may receive some help, but often the whole family needs help and be able to offer that is truly wonderful.

One of my favourite events DC Breathe created was our one-day retreats which were held at a beautiful castle in stunning grounds. These days were for ladies only, to come in comfy clothing and spend one day enjoying a beautiful lunch and have some quiet time.

Learning Reiki and Mindfulness, there were other classes throughout the day from outside providers, meditate in a sound bath, it was just amazing to see laughter, smiles and new friend-ship forming, incredible experience. DC Breathe have run several of these and will be looking in the future for locations abroad to allow people to truly relax.

I am pleased to say DC Breathe has been commissioned to complete a further 10-week project working with junior school students on their emotional wellbeing and as of March 2020 DC Breathe would of reached 20 schools in Ashford and Folkestone, over 250 students have attended the DC Breathe, 'WHO AM I'? course. I can easily say I am amazingly proud of this achieve-ment. My personal belief is, if we can get to the younger genera-tion and provide emotional and resilience tools at a young age, we will have a healthier young adult.

I am so proud of DC Breathe and what has been achieved so far. DC Breathe came runners up in Best new Business and won Best start up Business last December (2018), a day I will never forget. I can remember arriving at the hotel, hair styled to an inch of its life, sparkly dress that actually left glitter everywhere I went. Arriving at the welcome drinks, enjoying a glass of champagne, not knowing anyone and listening about all of their amazing companies and their back grounds and taking in all the excitable energies.

When it was time to take a seat, we were directed to our table and seeing my company on the table placement made my day, let alone winning. I can recall sitting down and watching my video of me talking about DC Breathe and what we have achieved on a massive screen In front of these 100s of people, feeling amazingly proud and how far the company had come.

When the nomination was read out for our category from a golden envelope and DC BREATHE was in the category I froze, then to hear the winners are DC Breathe I literally felt my feet were stuck to the floor. I felt like I was dreaming. My colleague was going crazy with excitement and I couldn't digest it. Whilst walking up onto the stage I was directed towards the microphone with a huge bright light directly at my face.

I don't know where my voice came from and to be honest, I don't even remember what I said, I am hoping I said something. Photos were taken and I was just in shock that we had achieved this. Our hard work has paid off, the long nights, long hours of work, planning had worked, other people believed in us.

My car was full of glitter from my glitter dress, and I just wanted to get home to show my family as they have been so supportive of me. I received beautiful hugs that night from so many people. It took me a good couple of days to process what has happened and to sit back and acknowledge just what DC Breathe had achieved.

Since then DC Breathe has received further commissioned work and carries on growing which I am forever grateful for. My colleague has left the company to pursue other employment and I wish them every success. I am excited to move the company forward especially after my eye-opening EFT matrix and 'Re-imprinting' course.

I discovered EFT through the ladies from my Reiki group at the Goddess rooms. I was unsure at the time if I could fit it in, as something always got in the way, I wasn't ready. Anyhow I checked the dates for an upcoming course, and it fitted in perfectly. So off to Brighton I went.

I was blown away how many people were on the course and how far they had travelled to be there, Italy, Spain, Germany and Ireland. I was absolutely blown away as it is still energy work, but the deep-rooted issue was being dealt with. EFT is Emotional Freedom Techniques and can be known as tapping as Tapping is involved. EFT calms the Amygdala gland (the fight or flight response) and removes energy blockages which can have a massive effect on someone's health.

The matrix re-imprinting is changing the belief of the event. Throughout the course I personally dealt with several issues and could not believe the difference in myself. I can now help with pain, addiction, phobias, depression and stress .

This is my journey so far, and I am grateful to everyone I have met and everything I have seen or dealt with as this has carved and created the person I am today. I am so excited to see who and what will come into my life next. I now have a clear mind and an open heart to truly discover my next journeys.

I would just like to acknowledge and thank a couple of people as I wouldn't be me without them.

I would like to thank my amazing parents Debbie and Mark for always supporting and helping me along my journey, love you both with all my heart.

I have to thank my beautiful friend Carly, who is truly my soul sister. We have been friends since we were at junior school and have shared so many memories together, happy and sad. Carly has rubbed my back whilst in labour and held me when I needed it. Carly is the one person I can always rely on, who I truly cherish x

I cannot name everyone who has helped and shared my life with me, I would like to thank everyone who has supported and guided me throughout my journey so far, love you all very much.

www.dcbreathe.com

Facebook - @Dcbreathe1 or DC Breathe- Emotional wellbeing for the mind and body by Donna Miller

Facebook – Desert Rose Reiki and Meditation

Instagram- donna.miller.92167

AUTHOR BIO

DONNA-MARIE MILLER

 Donna is many things, a mother, wife, daughter, aunt, cousin, friend, ex Police Officer, Emotional Wellbeing Coach, Qualified Mindfulness practitioner for Adults and Children, Qualified Eft matrix practitioner, drawing and talking therapist, Usui Reiki and Angelic Master and Director and owner of my award winner wellbeing company 'DC Breathe'.

Donna is a kind hearted person who loves making people smile and adores people who can makes her smile and allow her to laugh.

Donna loves travelling and meeting new people trying new foods and allowing her senses to go wild. Beauty is important to Donna in the sense of colour, smells and people, seeing life stories in their faces.

Donna can pick up on other energies very quickly and is always drawn to contagious beautiful smiles.

Donna's other passion and something she shares with her daughter Maisy is being creative. There is nothing she like best than sitting quietly with a pencil, paintbrush or a camera and capturing what she can see or imagining and bring it alive. This allows Donna time to switch off and simply be in that moment.

Donna's easiest and proudest achievements are her three beautiful children and her marriage to a wonderful kind-hearted man called Chris. Chris and Donna have been blessed with their twin boys Ashton and Ewan and their daughter Maisy.

Donnas house is full of children and animals who all have an important part in the family. In the house we have tears, laughter and the most amazing hugs and Donna wouldn't change it for the world.

Donna is an only child but comes from an amazing family. She is very close to her parents Mark and Debbie and to her 4 cousins Leeanne, Kelly, Michelle and Jemma who she sees as sisters due to the closeness in age and being brought up together.

Donna feels very lucky to have such inspirational people around her.

Donna's past careers have varied from being a Sales advisor, Travel agent to a 14-year career in the Police force as a Police officer.

Donna was a very different person then to the person writing this. Donna was stressed, tired, always felt she needed to prove herself, frustrated, confused, overwhelmed and hard in her personality as she needed to be in the police to deal with what you deal with.

Donna's life has changed so much she can easily and confidently say she does not recognise the person she described. Donna is still driven but in a different way, driven with compassion and confidence. Tiredness, overwhelmed, confused are no longer her.

She has embraced her kindness, gratitude which has allowed her to put down her hard barriers that she once had.

She can now see and think clearly to make choices from her gut and heart, not from what she thought was right. Donna life has changed since opening her eyes to Reiki and believing in her own gut instinct and allowing herself space and clarity to contemplate on choices and decisions with her heart.

www.dcbreathe.com

Facebook - @Dcbreathe1 or DC Breathe- Emotional wellbeing for the mind and body by Donna Miller

Facebook – Desert Rose Reiki and Meditation

 instagram.com/donna.miller.92167

7

IRINA VOSTORG

FREEDOM OF BEING THE RADIANT WOMAN

*M*y first memories as a child date back to the age of 2.5 years old. Honestly, I don't know whether these are my own memories or reconstructed from family stories. I see a girl sitting on the sand in the courtyard.

It is a hot sunny day in Morocco where her parents work as members of the Soviet Union support team on the construction of a plant. Both of them are caught at the doorway by the unexpected picture of their little girl – me – sitting and trying to play with a live scorpion.

The scorpion is going somewhere in the yard on his own purpose and the girl is stretching her hand to touch him and the distance between them is getting closer and closer by every second. My parents don't know what to do – to cry or to rush and hold the girl or to pray.

It is like a movie when time stops and all is sooooo slow. Finally..... The little finger and the scorpion don't meet. The scorpion moves forward and the girl is now in her parents' arms.

I guess these were my Guardian Angels and the Creator who settled all fine.

Next time I remember myself in the kindergarten being around 5-6 years old. Every day I was telling my parents the stories of a friendship between me and another girl in the group. She had a name and a surname, and we played a lot together. She was a great influence on me, and I was sharing with my parents what she had said about this and that and these were rather smart ideas.

They were so impressed that they finally decided to talk to the lady taking care of the group about this girl and her family. To their huge surprise there was no such girl in the group. Psychologists would call her an "imaginary friend". I know – she was – and still is – real. She is one of my guardian angels who was showing herself to me taking the image of a girl of my age.

In such a way my angels were telling me: *"You are not alone, we are close to you, we love you, we take care of you"*.

I was born in a country which no longer exists. Previously it was called the Soviet Union (USSR). My native city is Minsk, capital of Republic of Belarus. With my mom being Belarusian and my father Russian I spent 39 years in Minsk and then moved to Moscow, Russia, where I have been living for 11 years now.

Foreign languages were a routine in our family. My parents studied at the Linguistic University and spoke English, French and Italian. Both of them worked as interpreters for many years. Original books and music, listening to the Voice of America late at night in the kitchen, colleagues and business partners from Europe as guests in our home were features of my child and teenage years.

My mom and dad never went to London, Paris or Rome. They lived in the country where it was hard to travel abroad if you were not a member of the communist party. Later when the borders opened they did not have the money to travel.

I travelled to more than 40 countries on business and every time I went they were so proud of me looking forward to my stories of far away places.

English language, Russian literature and psychology have always been my passion. When at school I was a very quiet girl always with A+ marks and not many friends. Books were and still are my best friends.

Hours and hours spent, day and night reading everything: classical, modern, Russian, foreign, love, adventure, history, war, poems. My parents' home as well as my grandparents' was full of books. Like mine and our daughter's is now.

As for the English language – no wonder having been in the midst of foreign languages since early childhood I entered an English speaking school and started studying it at the age of 7.

The same with my younger brother who is now a successful businessman and a father.

I grew up being a shy, quiet and very sensitive child. I could easily feel the energies in the room, talking to people and even not talking. I was quite often absorbing peoples energy and then would be sick in bed.

I felt all problems and difficulties between my parents and did my best to be a peacemaker for them. Naturally years after their relations and my role as a savior were an issue of discussion during my sessions with different psychotherapists and healers.

Being rather lonely at school I had a bunch of friends in my local area. We explored the surroundings together and it was an incredible time to wonder around. When I was a teenager my genuine desire to explore life, to learn and to take risks, put me, on a couple of occasions in very very dangerous situations . I believe that my guardian angels were watching over me and saved me.

So, school was over, I left with the best marks and the Gold Medal – the appreciation for being the best pupil. I entered the same University as my parents – the Linguistic one and continued to learn languages.

By this time my mom had started leaning metaphysical stuff and our home library had a number of books on energy, karma, healing. She attended classes on energy healing. Remember it was the very beginning of 1990s and this was absolutely new to the former Soviet Union.

The Berlin wall was ruined in 1989, the Soviet Union was declared disintegrated in 1991 and the new opportunities started to come. My mom's intention was to have access to the Source, to the Creator, however she was never baptised. Neither was I. I went to the orthodox church and was baptised at my own will when I was in my mid-twenties.

At 21 I got married and within 3 years we had a baby. A little girl, who is now 26 and part of my team in the company.

My knowledge of English helped me to get a part time job in international projects of foreign journalists. They represented USA Today, Paris Match, The Observer and were arriving to the young country of Belarus to report politics, economy and culture. I did the job of a PA and interpreter. That was an incredibly great experience which put me in the offices of the President of the country, the Cabinet of Ministers, top managers and influencers.

Everything in my life looked good – I was married, had a daughter, had a great job with a good salary, but at the same time in myself I was feeling unhappy and empty. I had the feeling as if something was missing and I could not figure out exactly what it was. I had soul pain and a strange feeling that my life might finish soon.

So in 1995 this happened – I was in a car accident and had a "near death experience".

I was sitting behind the driver in a Ford micro bus which was driving us back from the Paralympic games in Germany. I was an interpreter for the Belarus team performing at the Paralympics. It was raining, we were in Poland rushing to get home in Minsk. I was fastened in the same as everybody else and we were all napping.

The sound of the rain, quiet music playing, it was a long ride and all of a sudden I unfastened my belt. Why? I don't know. I continued to nap, and I heard the voice right in my head: *"Fasten your seat belt!"* I opened my eyes, all of my fellow passengers were sleeping, not one of them could have said it.

I closed my eyes again without fastening the belt. *"Fasten the belt!"* I heard this voice in my head louder and more insistent. I ignored it. *"FASTEN THE BELT NOW!"* The voice was shouting at me, but I did not make a move with me eyes closed. A minute or so later I heard the crash, the noise, everything was turning around, shouts, pain, darkness.

It was only later that I realised my angels were doing their best to save me.

I still remember myself looking down from the height of 10-15 meters to the earth. I saw there was a girl on the ground just off the road, with her eyes closed. Some people were walking around, there was a car near a big tree. A police and an ambulance car. Raining. Peace.

Suddenly I realised the girl on the ground is ME. So quiet. Not moving. And I realised the one who is observing all of this is also me. So quiet. So peaceful. There was no pain. I felt so much love and beauty and peace. Somehow I knew that this was the end of my physical life. It was a bit strange, but fine.

All of a sudden I thought: "Oh our daughter! How would she live without me?" I knew that she had a loving father and grandparents from both sides and she would be ok. At the same time, I felt so lonely as if I was going to miss something very-very important.

She was only 2 years old and my death meant that I would not see her growing and going to the kindergarten and school. I would not see her enjoying life, not able to hug and kiss her, not teaching her and sharing my thoughts with her. Part of me knew that she would be completely ok, loved and cherished and cared for.

I knew that I would take care of her from the sky. But I thought of the EXPERIENCE, of the physical experience of being together that was literally no longer with me. I remember myself shouting loud: "Put me back! I command you to return me back! I want to be alive!" Well, I believe I was not really shouting loud into the sky but I had a very strong feeling that I did.

Then again it was all quiet and dark and white and empty and again white and more white and light everywhere. I saw big white figures, darkness, the feeling of being inside and outside of a tube, everything going so fast.

When I opened my eyes the first thing I saw was the crucifix of the Christ. I was in bed in a white hospital room and the crucifix was just in front of my eyes, a bit higher. It was so quiet in the room however there were other beds around. All of a sudden I started saying aloud in Russian the Our Father prayer. I didn't even know that I knew the words:

Our Farther, which art in heaven,

Hallowed be thy name;

Thy kingdom come;

Thy will be done in earth as it is in heaven.

Give us this day our daily bread;

And forgive us our trespasses

As we forgive those who trespass against us;

And lead us not into temptation,

But deliver us from the evil one.

Amen

I read this prayer 3 times aloud not taking my eyes from the crucifix, then closed them and fell asleep. I knew that my prayer to be returned back to the Earth was heard and fulfilled. I was grateful.

I am still grateful every day for the life I have here on Earth. For more than 25 years my mornings start with the words and feeling of gratitude. I am so blessed and happy to be alive and to live with my loved ones.

It took me a while to recover after the traffic accident. I spent some time in the Polish hospital and I believe that was really a blessing to be taken to this hospital where I saw the crucifix on the wall and could pray. Then another hospital in my home country with a lot of medications. The left part of my face and head was cut by the window glass in the car and it took some time to recover.

This event happened in 1995 and many years after I leant that the beginning and middle of the 1990s were years of mass awakening. I knew that something had changed in my life during and after this experience, but I was still asleep spiritually. It took me more than 10 years to achieve the next step of my personal awakening.

What was I doing during those 10 years? I was a wife and a mother and worked a lot, really a lot, being a top manager. After our daughter turned 3 years old she started going to kindergarten, the place where she stayed for half of the day first.

I would take her there early in the morning; she was not very enthusiastic about staying in a group of children, but I had to work. In the middle of 1990s the economic situation in the former Soviet Union was not easy and we needed a salary form of both of us – my ex-husband and me.

Later our daughter started going for the full day at the kindergarten and I was working a full day in the office. That was the usual story of a working mum and wife who was spending 8-9 hours in the office 5 days a week, 2 hours a day going there and back home using public transport, and then doing all house-keeping work at home in the evening and weekends.

We never had anybody to help around the house and all cleaning, cooking, laundry and grocery shopping were part of my everyday routine in addition to a highly demanding job. I was very quickly promoted in the office and was opening new business lines, activities, markets for one company and afterwards for another one.

On the one hand I was very satisfied and fulfilled – I had a personal office, a top position, new big apartment in a nice area, and finally a personal office car. Regular business trips to New York, Singapore, London, Baden-Baden, Munich, Rome, Milan, Monte-Carlo and other amazing cities, staying in 5 star hotels, gaining successful contracts that were bringing good profit to the company.

During these trips I met hundreds of new people, learnt a lot about the world called the Earth and investigated and experienced life. On the other hand, I had a strange feeling of sadness and emptiness inside as if I was missing something and even I did not know what it was I was missing. Sometimes I had a feeling of a hole inside my chest.

I did not want to replace the emptiness by smoking or alcohol. I never drank or smoked which may seem unusual as I had grown up in an environment where somebody always smoked or drank. When I was a teenager I gave myself a word not to smoke until the age of 12.

When I turned 12 I told myself that I would keep this promise until the age of 14. Then I repeated the same at 14, 16 and 18. By the age of 20 I felt that I was free from the desire to drink or smoke. I am 50 years old and have never smoked a cigarette and feel good about that.

Instead of drinking or smoking I went shopperholic.

This addiction looks more or less normal something like *"Oh we girls LOVE shopping!"* But in reality I didn't enjoy it. I was buying clothes, sometimes not even opening the bags at home and never wearing the stuff. The moment of *"I LOVE IT"* was a short moment of paying the bill, but by this time I could afford it. I did not know that I was trying to fill in a very-very empty place deep in my soul. What was I looking for? What sort of love?

Was I happy? No. But I was scared to acknowledge that, not only to people but even to myself. My life looked so good – family, work, appearance, money. But one day I had to tell the truth.

Our daughter became a teenager and the hard times began. In my childhood I was a very quiet teenager, I was not a rebel or problem creator. I was too worried about the happiness and peace of my parents and was afraid of bringing them any trouble. I had no idea how to deal with a teenager who turned to be abso-lutely the opposite of being a nice girl.

I felt at a loss and finally one autumn evening went to the clinic, knocked at the door of psychotherapist and said that I needed help with our daughter. The woman looked at me and asked 3 questions: *"Are your married?"* – *"Yes"*, *"Are you happy?"* –

"No", "Do you understand that first you have to work on your own issues?" – "Yes".

So that was the start of my personal therapy which I had weekly for more than a year with one expert, then I continued with another one, then another one and I am still attending my personal sessions once a week.

Meanwhile I was attending personal coaching programs for life and business. For 13 years I have been taking regular sessions from experts on soul, body and mind to help me understand and heal my wounds and traumas, to find my path and live a happy life. Did I succeed? Things are much better now, and I am still on my way.

Today I am writing this chapter under a powerful oak tree on a pond shore. All this beauty is in the park just across the corner from my apartment in Moscow. The megapolis is full of beautiful parks and I am so blessed to live in a place full of greenery, fresh air, walking and bicycle paths. I go there for a walk, meditations, clearing my mind, to cry, to relax, to talk to the Creator practically every day.

Today is a warm July day and I love July which is my birthday month. It has been raining heavily in the morning and now the sky is extremely blue and clear. I am looking around and my eyes rest on huge birch and oak trees. The water in the pond reflects the sky and there are ducks softly floating there. So peaceful and quiet and only 20 minutes by car to the very centre of Moscow where I have my company's office.

11 years ago, I moved to Moscow by the invitation of a large financial company. I was offered a top management position and felt so happy! I had a new apartment with the rent paid by the company, a very high salary, nice people around me, shareholders appreciating my work, multiple business trips all over the world.

I had a strong feeling that I had opened a new chapter in my life, I was much happier and fulfilled. I started attending every live seminars and workshops that were available. Moscow had then, and still has thousands of options to study every day and night for everybody. I was literally hungry for studying!

My choice were courses on femininity, discovering the inner Goddess, sexuality, yoni healing, dao, tantra, yoga, psychology, life coaching, spiritual practices of different schools, intuition, archetypes, shamanism, men-women relations, sacred geometry, astrology, Taro, numerology, brain activity, massage, arts, vocal, dancing, crystals, candle magic, palm reading, Mandala dance, kabbala, angels, Ericson hypnosis, system-vector psychology, aromatherapy, candle therapy, symbolon, initiation therapy for men and women, reincarnation, walking on fire, meditations in water, etc.

Strange as this may seem I was very quickly having the feeling "I know that" after learning some new modality or technique. I had a feeling as if I had always known, forgot and later woken up and remembered.

One night I woke up and sat in my bed. On the wall in front of me I saw white symbols, words in an unknown language, they were going from the ceiling to the floor. I was sitting in my bed looking at these lines and could not tell the language although I am a linguist. However somehow deep in my soul I KNEW it and knew the meaning of the text. I absorbed it all and fell asleep with a conscious knowledge that I had been given some important message in the language of LIGHT.

I began Cosmo energy classes and became Bachelor in this spiritual modality, later Master and Teacher in Reiki, Kundalini Reiki, Moon Reiki and many more modalities of Reiki, I practiced more than 16 of different energy approaches, Magnetic Heart Activations and Cellular Light Body activations taken on a monthly basis for 3 years.

I graduated a life coaching program in the Fowlers Wainwright International Academy and was extremely happy to get a number of coaching instruments. I studied psychology in addition to my University diplomas of interpreter and foreign languages teacher and my MBA in economy.

It was quite a challenge for me – to work hard in the office and to spend each night after work at new or continuing class. Each weekend I attended spiritual courses and took a number of retreats to beautiful places during vacations including India twice and Nepal.

No surprisingly I was losing interest in the office work which, in fact, it was just providing me with a living and was a way to pay for all these great classes that cost a lot of money. I was asking: "Creator, please help me to change that!" At the beginning of my spiritual path I was not aware that you have to be very specific asking Creator to change something in your life. I was not specific, honestly, I didn't even know what it was exactly I wanted to change.

One day THE CHANGE came and the very moment I heard the bell to my door (literally) I knew that was the answer to my prayers. It was an early cold winter morning. The stress and shock and fear that I experienced on that day and continued to face many months after brought huge changes in my life. Finally, I took a decision to quit the company and start my own activity as a personal coach and group teacher.

I am very grateful to the shareholders who understood me and supported me. Many years have passed, and we still have a good relationship. One day a former shareholder told me: "I highly respect you Irina, you are a very brave woman. You are an inspiration for me. Sometimes when I face a challenging task I tell myself – she managed, I will as well". This is huge compliment for me, from a person with huge business and life experiences. I am extremely grateful for the Creator to have put me in an environment of respectful and kind people.

It's easy to say – I will start my own activity – but hard for me to fulfill. No matter how many classes as a student I had taken I felt I was not good enough, scared to openly call myself a teacher, a clairvoyant, a coach. Day by day, class by class I was overcoming my fears, my hesitations, my inner dialogue, not always supportive to myself. As soon as the class started I always felt very protected and supported as if somebody was talking through me it. I was and still am in the flow connected to the Creator.

After a while in my private practice I was offered a position in one of the largest personal development centers for women in Moscow. In 2009 I went there as a student and took all of the available classes and there were dozens of them. I was going deeper and deeper in the world of femininity, men-women relations, energy.

In the beginning of 2011, I became a teacher there and travelled throughout Russia with 2 days seminars and evening workshops 2 times a month, giving classes at the Moscow office in between. I met thousands of wonderful women and was doing my best to help them heal their wounds and find answers to their questions.

That was the time when I was listening to hundreds of women's personal stories and my heart was crying over many of them. I was asking myself and the Creator how could it be that women were suffering so much. I heard stories of abuse and hatred, of losing hope and desire to live, of despair and addictions, of loneliness and betrayal.

I met women of different ages and social status, all of them being united in one aim – to find answers to their questions and ways of a better, healthier, happier life. Many of them were looking for their life mission and I spent hours giving personal sessions and helping them.

I worked in this place for 3 years as a group trainer and personal psychologist and am very grateful to the owner and all the staff.

Many of my former colleagues have their own private businesses now and we remain friends.

When I was working in the corporate business and travelling abroad I was always looking at women in different countries with huge interest. The way they walk, talk, live. From each trip I would return with paintings or small statuettes of local women. I did not know why I was doing this, but my eyes were looking for them everywhere. Later on, I realised that I was gathering my women circle.

The circle of women who share the same feelings, who are the one, my Tribe. I have found them, here in Russia and abroad. I thank Tina Pavlou for the amazing feeling of being at home, with MY Tribe. "Welcome to the tribe, baby" – Tina's words are still in my ears from the moment we met in Switzerland.

Do you remember that I love reading? There are writers whose books influenced me a lot. When moving flats, the first and most precious thing to pack is my library with hundreds of books. I will skip some Russian authors names here in this chapter however as they are numerous and just mention some of the international ones, writing about spiritual and psychological issues.

They help me to find my way and are my compass. I am highly grateful and bless for their books: Neale Donald Walsh, Sonia Choquette, Barbara Ann Brennan, Bruce Wilkinson, Kryon, John Gray, Eric Berne, Robert Leahy, Diane Stein, Judith Bennett, Danielle Blackwood, Elaine St.James, Barbara Sher,

Rhonda Byrne, Robin Sharma, Richard Bach, Paulo Coelho, Osho, Deepak Chopra, Joe Vitale, Lise Bourbeau, Louise Hay, Julia Cameron, Doreen Virtue, Drunvalo Melchizedek, Gay Hendricks, Don Miguel Ruiz, Michael Berg, Shakti Gawain, Agapi Stassinopoulos, Murry Hope, Sharron Rose, Jean Shinoda Bolen, Cherry Gilchrist, Clarissa Pinkola Estes, Vianna Stibal, Eckhart Tolle, Marina Borruso, Yehuda Berg, Michael Berg, Karen Berg, Tina Pavlou and collaboration.

I still love walking in my favourite park near my home every day, talking to trees and bushes, walking deep in the woods no matter what the weather. I spend hours there. This park remembers my tears and grief when my dad passed away in 2011 after lung cancer. I was shouting at the Creator: *"Why? Why? That is not fair! Why did not you help me to heal him???"*

We were very close dad and me. We celebrated our birthdays together, mine being the 11th July and his on the 14th July. It was the middle of March 2011 when my dad very delicately told me via Skype that he had some lungs issues I KNEW that he would pass away soon. I was crying: *"Please daddy please NO!"* By this time, we had resolved all of our misunderstandings, and I was planning to enjoy some time of peaceful father-daughter relations, but his Soul had a different plan.

We definitely had a contract with my dad on me helping to become a healer. Since being a young girl, I was praying for the health of my father. He drank and smoked a lot. There were other members of the family with alcohol and nicotine addictions. I remember myself going to the orthodox church every few days and praying for my dad to stop drinking. Hours and days of praying, in the church and at home.

When I later became interested in different healing modalities I worked on my father and he was open and willing. When I learnt about his cancer I knew I should continue to studying healing and do my best to heal him.

But his Soul chose to pass away and it took me several years to heal my own wounds blaming myself for not being able to save him. My cousin died of cancer as well and some of my help was appreciated. I pray for them. Of course, I know now that I cannot save anybody. I can only help if the person chooses to wake up and live and enjoy life. With my experience of being human I have forgotten how it feels to let the person be who he/she is. I am still learning the process to remember, accept and respect such a choice.

The modality that made a huge impact on my life, which helped to put the puzzle together was theta healing. My deep gratitude to Vianna Stibal and her family, my teachers and fellow students and more than 1600 students whom I have taught in this modality during the last 6 years.

My beautiful park plays its role in this story. By autumn 2013 I was deeply exhausted by the everyday work with clients, numerous travels, teaching live seminars, little sleep, difficult family relations. I was going through a personal crisis finding myself lonely, lost and weak. I felt my aura full of low vibrational energy, I could not clean my blocks and was absorbing too much of other people's thoughts and feelings. I took the decision to leave the job in centre for women and to start a new activity. What activity? I did not know but trusted the Creator.

Day after day I was walking for hours in my favourite park asking for signs and help. One day I started hearing in my mind words that soon were making poems. All of them began with the line "The light shining from heaven I pass through myself". After that there were other lines, there were many!

So many of them I could not remember! I was feeling hungry, tired, cold under the rain and wind, but the lines were going on and on and I could not leave the park. The same went on the next day and the next one after that. The only things that I remembered were the beautiful words of the light from heaven. I was asking Creator what that meant but as a reply I was only hearing this line in my mind: "The light shining from heaven I pass through myself".

After several days of these walks in the park I woke up during the night – I saw the word THETA HEALING in my dream. I did not know the word. In the morning I opened google and to my great surprise I found that there was a modality. I checked for some teachers in Moscow, registered for the nearest class and on November 6rd 2013 received my first theta healing practitioners certificate.

My first class notebook was full of poems, I had a strong feeling that I was in the right place, feeling the right energy and that something extremely important and life changing was happening that very moment. Since that day I have taken more than 60 classes on theta healing, both in Russia and abroad, many of them for 2-3-4-5 times.

Out of these 60 classes I had 34 classes directly from Vianna Stibal, the founder of the modality. I was her interpreter into Russian at some of the classes, part of international teams hosting Vianna in different countries.

In 2015 I received the level of Master Certificate of Science of theta healing which is the highest degree. In 2017 I opened my LLC in Moscow with the office and training room in the very centre of Moscow. Since 2014 I have given about 160 classes of theta healing as a teacher and am blessed to have some incredible students learning to live their lives and follow their personal paths. The name of my company is "Academy of Irina Vostorg "The Radiant Woman" ltd and the slogan is "The light shining from heaven I pass through myself".

This chapter would not be complete without the story of my relationship with my ex-husband. It was my decision to divorce, even though everything looked so good. I was not happy and was not following my path. It took me several years to get the divorce. I left everything and started earning money to build a new life here in Moscow. It has taken time and effort, but it was all worth it.

The feeling of being free, following MY WAY is so much more fulfilling! I remained friends with my ex and he was and is the best father for our daughter. He was my karmic partner for 25 years and I am grateful for all the experiences and learning we both have had.

Our daughter plays an important role in my company being my PA and she is my student in Kundalini Reiki. She performed a lot of English-Russian and Russian-English translations of theta healing manuals and is part of my soul family. Nearly a quarter of a century ago I asked Creator to return me back to the Earth to enjoy life with my daughter and here it is!

I am now in loving relationship with my partner and we both pass through different moments, helping one another to heal the traumas and enjoy life. I am grateful for our experiences many happy and some, not so happy days – they all are true blessings for our souls.

My mother and my brother and his family are members of my soul family, we support, respect and love one another. My mom being 75+ still has a huge interest in life, she holds my back and is my greatest fan. My mentors, coaches, psychotherapists, teachers, healers have been of incredible value to my life. These people have helped me to remember who I AM.

I feel so very blessed to be going further in my life. Being 50 is a new experience for me and I have started to enjoy it. I am looking forward to studying Angelic Reiki, business development, fashion and style, and enjoying more music and dancing and sports. Life here on the Earth looks like an adventure and it is my choice what sort of adventure I create.

It was not an easy job for me to write this chapter, especially in a language which is not my native one. There were days and weeks when I was feeling completely empty, lost, asking myself and Creator the question "What should I write? Why should I write?"

At these moments I was opening "The Complete Conversations with God" by Neale Donald Walsch, I would sit reading and thinking. Now I know the answer. I want to bring a difference to the world and that doesn't sound too much for me now. My mission is to help women feel their true shine and glory, remember their greatness and live their personal life of a Radiant Woman.

AUTHOR BIO

IRINA VOSTORG

Irina is the founder and CEO of Academy of Irina Vostorg "The Radiant Woman" Ltd, the registered trademark company in Moscow, Russia.

She is an interpreter, MBA, psychologist, life coach, healer, Reiki Master and Theta Healing Certificate of Science Instructor, motivational speaker, expert on Russian TV.

In her beautiful office in the very center of Moscow you can see Irina's paintings on the walls, feel the warm and homelike atmosphere and are treated like a dear guest.

Irina was born on 11th July 1969 in Belarus and has been living in Moscow for 11 years.

She is now experiencing being 50 earth years old with grace and joy looking for new soul opportunities.

She is ready to share her knowledge and inspire women of 45+ to live a fulfilled life radiating light and energy.

Irina is the author of more than 15 workshops and seminars for women.

She loves her family where 2 ginger cats are fully-fledged members along with human beings. Both of the cats are foundlings and are true blessings.

Irina's personal slogan is "Live! Breathe! Shine!" and she is looking forward to sharing her taste of life with thousands of people here in Russia and abroad.

As she speaks fluent English she is open to teach theta healing and other modalities as well as offer personal sessions live and online both in Russian and English.

Contact:

Email: info@irinavostorg.ru
Website: www.irinavostorg.ru

YouTube: https://www.youtube.com/
channel/UCEVpH9XxGXrz21MjFoUpYVQ

facebook.com/irina.vostorg

instagram.com/irinavostorg.ru

youtube.com/UCEVpH9XxGXrz21MjFoUpYVQ

My earliest memory of being different was around age four or five. I started to realise that I had the ability to read people and situations and energy, and it became scary for me because I would think about something happening, and it would happen.

This was intuition at an early age, the ability to anticipate how people would behave based on signs I was able to read in their behaviour. It was as if I could insert myself into people's thoughts by sensing their energy and vibrations, by intuiting everything about them they were giving off through their mood, face, body language, and so on.

I realised quite quickly that I was different. I realised that this ability to read people and understand them and anticipate their behaviour was a special skill, and something of an obligation. I realised, even at the age of 5, that I had been given this skill not only to serve myself, but to help others.

About the same time in my life, I was also empowered by a particular situation in which I was split - physically, mentally, and emotionally — while being involved in the middle of an argument between two people. One person was calling me into a room to help them, and the other person was telling me to go away, to protect me.

The situation was traumatic and I won't bear too many of the details, but it was a watershed moment in my life that proves to me that I have value: value beyond people who do not understand my worth, value beyond a world that wants to push and pull me in its own directions and for its own agendas, and value to transcend adversity and bring illumination and encouragement to a confused, disconnected, and broken world.

At age seven, I vividly remember having a conversation with my father about my life. He was a slave of sorts to his company, his life dominated by the needs and whims of his bosses. I remember talking with him about this one day, and in his pride, he discounted my words, telling me that I should one day become a barrister (or, "Attorney" in American language) because I had an answer for everything, and would never back down. I asked him what he meant, and he told me that I would have to go to university to become an attorney and earn the position.

I replied, "I'm never going to university because I do not want to end up like you. I'm not going to grow up to become a slave to other people. On the contrary, those people are going to pay me to help them".

After this conversation, I set the intention of becoming an entrepreneur, birthing a crystal focus on my future. I knew the traditional education route was not for me, and I did not set my hope or sense of security on obtaining a degree and entering the job market in the traditional sense.

I didn't just want to learn one person's perspective and become a slave to it. I wanted to create a world for myself, even though I was too young to truly know what that meant. I just knew I wanted it. I wasn't going to be put in a box; I was going to make the box.

I didn't want to devote my life to simply memorising and remembering things other people had done; I wanted to be a creator. I wanted to produce something new. I knew I was capable of creating my own world in the world I lived in.

Not surprisingly, conversations like these led to me feeling isolated and disconnected from family around me, even as a child. I felt alone in my world, a world bubbling with the power to read and discern people's intentions and manifest things quickly. It was a confusing place to be.

When I was 13 years old, my parents divorced. This was the first time I genuinely felt split from everything to do with family. It was as if my whole life had been built on a foundation of inconsistency and what felt like lies.

Very shortly after this, I tried to commit suicide. It was of course deeply traumatic, but that event oriented me to realise that there's more to life than what I had thought, that I was worth more than what the world's lies said, and that I was meant to be a force of power and truth in the world. I had skills and experience and a desire to change people's lives. I realised I hadn't been given all of these things, these precious gifts, for nothing.

At the age of 16 I left home and left school. I was alone. But shortly after, I met someone who recognised what I had to offer. My paths crossed with a recruitment consultant, and she asked me what my plans were. I told her that I was interested in hairdressing because I had done it for a while. I remember it vividly: she said to me, "You want more than this. I can tell".

While I was deeply inspired and moved by her energy, the energy in her office, and the big dreams she set for me, I started on a journey of power, a journey fuelled not by my desire to live who I was, but a journey controlled by a need to prove everyone else wrong. I went on to build somewhat of a small empire, a fantastic business career in which I succeeded, yet one which left my true self lacking. I was helping people, still, and doing much of what I wanted to do, but without the right structures and strategies in place.

I built a seven-figure consulting business in some of the world's most complex, male-dominated, technical environments. Though I didn't claim to be an academic, I was in an academic environment serving others and helping them grow, so much so that I forgot about building my own life.

I was building infrastructure and energy projects for others and consulting on how the should grow yet neglecting much of the perfect energy within me to guide me where I needed to go personally. I was constantly trying to give people the fulfilment I needed for myself.

I aimed to help people find security, connection, great opportunities for their own careers, and so on. I started doing this outside of the business context as well, and I continued manifesting relationships with people who weren't the best for me, as I was seeking connection and trust and love, yet missing myself in the midst of all of it.

This led to a lot of self-medication, destructive behaviour, and all of the other crazy things that find a person when they can't find themselves. The self-program and subconscious talk I had created inside my own mind were simply not serving me, and I was going down a spiral path. Consciously, I knew I was meant for more. But the system had gotten me, and I was in a matrix of lies, half-truths, and despair.

Not only this, my father had passed away just as I was getting started, and this led to a great deal of regret as I couldn't prove to him that I had become the person I said I would become. I regretted leaving home. I regretted many of my decisions as a teenager.

I just regretted, and this dominated my psyche for too long. I had built a big empire filled with homes and cars and nice things, but one day at 29 I woke up and realised the world was empty. The world was different. It needed to change. And it did change.

It was as if a veil was lifted at that point in my life, and I began to see things and myself, as they really were. Even though everything I had been doing was coming from a good place, I realised I didn't like who I was. I was surrounded by the wrong people. I was doing the wrong things in the right way, and it was all wrong for me. I was looking for love outside of myself, because I didn't know what self-love meant.

A few months later I met with a specialist and was told that I would have trouble conceiving because of my hormone levels. I decided to have my eggs frozen. But I was told this would not work. This rattled me because I had been socially conditioned by my dad to believe that I needed to become married in order to have children. And so, in November 2013, I married.

Three days after our wedding, on the first day of my fertility window, I became pregnant with my son, Skyler. I was divorced in 2015, which was one of the most challenging things I had ever done. The relationship was not right, and I didn't want my son to be around parents who were not in alignment. I quickly became a single parent to ensure my son didn't experience his younger years as I did. Both Skyler and I are grateful that he has an amazing father who supports him, my work and journey in life.

I continued to seek validation, love, and security and things outside of me, which led to a great awakening in my story.

Being forced to make decisions for another human being caused me to look deeply inside myself. I had to determine what my mission was, what kind of parent I wanted to be, what kind of son I hoped Skyler would become.

The career I had adopted had given me wonderful skills, but I realised it wouldn't help me leave the legacy I wanted to leave, for myself and for Skyler. I noticed how desperately unhappy people were in business, life and their careers, and it took me back to my childhood in a strange way.

I realised I was working with the very type of people I didn't want to become, people who had been running a race and climbing ladder after ladder only to reach their destinations unfulfilled and insecure. And I couldn't truly empower them because I could not embrace their broken dreams.

These people were in a world of ego and competitiveness and drive, but they had never been taught to communicate or connect and do the most empowering things human beings can do with each other. They had never been taught how to build deep human relationships, how to build great and functional corporate cultures, how to create an environment of trust and psychological safety and purpose.

I was desperate to show this very scientific and academic world that these truths of self-empowerment, transcendence, and energy are not in conflict with a scientific and technical paradigm. In fact, they flow from our neurology, and are as scientific as anything else, able to be quantified and measured, but often dismissed.

One of my missions was to help bridge these two worlds of science and spirituality, to prove that they are perfectly co-existent and interdependent and co-functional. I was convinced that if people understood that these two are together and not distant, they would truly create things that would change the world.

This took me full circle and put me on a mission to look deep inside the gifts I had been given, the skills and experiences and love in my own heart and reorient it toward creating these very things that were lacking in the people I was serving. I realised I needed to serve people differently, understanding their vastly different and unique needs for growth. Every person, team, business and challenge is different.

I have created a programme that enables people to tap into their own genius, their personal power of authenticity. I help enable them co-create as a team to develop or find the solutions to their own challenges in life or business.

I facilitate and co-create as part of their team, with them, to help them define and then live by their highest values and purpose in life first, remove their subconscious beliefs, biases and judgements, and then become leaders of others in doing the same.

I have a formula which taps into the subconscious mind, removes limiting beliefs, and aligns one's values and purpose to their career or business. This methodology shows them how to structure their business and the roles in it to the right people, how to attract, recruit, coach and retain those who are on the same mission as the business, and collectively ride the challenges that will come with the right support. This creates the true exponential growth that companies dream about.

We create a culture of connection, co-creation, communication where Physiological safety and Flow Psychology are at the heart of everything we do. This starts with the individual first: their consciousness and personal power by mastering their mind, finding their purpose, getting clear on their value system and unleashing their ability to lead themselves first before co-creation, and leading others.

When I began these efforts, when I started learning and taking my new journey, opening my mind to the world of neuroscience and the psychology of human connection and trust. I collected information and followed my intuition to build a groundswell of knowledge around conscious cultures, trying to understand what makes truly great organisations thrive well. I kept following my intuition and blended the philosophical, practical, and biochemical elements of these items into a set of theories that were very pure and resonated from within me.

And this was the final moment in my transformation, realising that the great work I had set out to do in the lives of others was intended for me to do on myself, to find who I really was.

I always instinctively knew that I didn't want to specialise in simply one area of human behaviour. I found all of it fascinating and knew that it all had different roles to play in determining who a person is, and I wanted to master and understand the process completely.

As I was undergoing my awakening, I realised that one of the reasons I didn't want to go the university route at the beginning is because I felt that they would teach me something foreign or different about human behaviour, theories that would just corner me into their way of thinking, and stifle me from exploring my own understanding of human behaviour.

Yet while I had rejected the idea of becoming a prisoner of someone else's mind in the educational sense, I realised I had become a prisoner to wrong ways of thinking in other areas of my life. This is what prompted me to truly break into an awakening.

Part of my awakening was having faith that the rabbit holes I was exploring were going to come together to help me produce an entirely new way of understanding others. I was building a new paradigm for how to manifest connection, trust, and collective consciousness to build great teams, and I was beginning to stand in power.

Here, I would be able to help others, and help myself as much. I had to keep faith on the journey I was on, driven by the need for genuine self-love. When you don't have self-love, you have nothing, and committing to rebuilding yourself requires focus and dedication. I realised so much of my life had been operating from a place of survival, as no one had ever taught me how to thrive. And it was time to thrive.

I refused to operate any longer from a place of fear and lack and scarcity, from the lower mind, from a place of little. I was done operating from a place where I craved connection but didn't even know how connection worked. I was done helping people pursue their vain dreams of status and titles and advancement which were only being used as futile attempts for connection and significance and validation, and I was building a new power instead.

I brought these new principles of collective consciousness and trust and authentic human connection into a void in the educational and leadership development industry, and I built these practices for myself before showing them to others. This is where the Science of Superhuman was born. This was the beginning of my spiritual awakening.

I had just severed a highly dysfunctional professional relationship with a woman whose business I had helped build, and she had negatively affected not only myself, but my son as well. This led me to another portion of my awakening, timeline therapy. In this therapy I realised that much of my negative subconscious programming had come from my experiences as a child.

I had grown up in an environment where there was a great amount of secrets and distrust and lack of communication. I had grown up in an environment in which people didn't talk, they just exploded after emotions had built up over time. Timeline therapy helped me realise that I had negatively blamed myself, and had layered myself with guilt and shame, identifying myself this way as a result of growing up.

In no way do I blame anyone for this, our parents do the best they can with the information and subconscious programming they are also given, however, this experience has driven me to create the Science of Superhuman and also a movement which will include conscious parenting. Healing ourselves is the only way to ensure we do not pass on our trauma unconsciously.

When I realised that I had taken the label of love away from my life and had only identified with guilt and shame and was free to empower myself back to a label of love, I felt an energy surge through my body, from my head to my feet. I felt the negative energy release from me, from my torso all the way up, and positive energy and a wave of joy replace it, filling my upper body.

My mental fog was lifted, and my sense of purpose was augmented amplified, a total replacement of energy and myself. I was healing inside even as I was learning something new about what I wanted to give the world, an awakening out of pain and an awakening into purpose.

It's hard to explain, but I felt something like the opposite of a panic attack: an endless cascade of positive emotions as I realised why I was how I was, and how I was changing into something new. The negative programming started to be cleared away, and positive truths, one truth after another, replaced it. I had a rebirth. I was the same person, but new. Little did I know the inner work had only just begun, but I had never been so appreciative of every experience gained throughout my whole life.

I began communicating my truth: human consciousness is so much more than the limits we put on it. The potential for what human consciousness, especially when blended with others, can become, is inexhaustible. I had been sent here to show people the power of consciousness, performance, communication, co-creation, and how to control these things by understanding how different parts of the brain work.

I was passionate about creating the highest performing teams in the world and showing leaders how to embody these principles. I wanted to help people build cultures of thriving in psychological safety and trust. And I was finally becoming who I needed to be in order to tell others how what they needed to know.

This was my awakening, and more importantly, this is my awakening. This is who I am, fears and all, past and all, history and all, scars and all. All of me is meant to become something more than who I am in this moment, more than just the now and more than the limitations of our 5 senses.

I am a person healing, and a person healed. I am a person growing, and a person grown. I am for others, and I am for myself, to heal my wounds and to heal others. I am not who I was, and I am not yet fully who I will become, but I am who I am meant to be. And in this I rest.

In a world that is trying to sell you technology, someone else's process, systems or social idealisms of what success is, I am obsessed with the human mind and raising our consciousness, showing you how to strip away everything that isn't really you.

Master your mind, find your purpose, unleash your inner genius and redefine leadership. When you build businesses and a life from this place of being you leave the world a better place than when you came here. That to me is your legacy.

Jennifer Evans is a woman complete, and a woman changing.

She has carved a niche across multiple industries as the Human Accelerator, and she's a dynamic speaker, writer, and thinker whose research on human consciousness, neuroscience, and conscious cultures has helped thousands of leaders.

But before her work, and more importantly, behind it, she is a soul made strong by a life of great adversity and greater overcoming. She has helped many leaders walk-through the pain and journeys she herself has walked and has manifested resilient compassion through it.

Jennifer's passion is to help organisations create environments of ultimate performance through psychological safety, connection, co-creation, conscious leadership and culture meaning unbridled human potential is inevitable.

She's interested in blending the intricacies of transcendent human energy with the mechanics of neurochemistry and behavioural psychology in the quest for peak human performance, and peak human connection.

She is someone who has been to the deepest valleys of the human experience and emerged true and awakened, someone who has learned to heal herself and thus serve others.

Contact:

Linked in - https://www.linkedin.com/in/humanaccelerator/

Website – Humanaccelerators.com

 facebook.com/thehumanaccelerator

 instagram.com/jennifer.l.evans

9

JULIE TAYLOR

I can remember having a discussion with one of my girls a few years ago about having a 'not fitting in' gene and that in the future it would have a name – because I know a lot of people feel that they just don't fit into this world.

From a very young age I was utterly convinced I must be adopted – how did I come to be a part of this family? I didn't fit! I didn't think I was like any of the others, it was only as I grew that I realised there was a physical resemblance – so I must be a part of this family!

Born in Dulwich Hospital, the youngest child of six, my sister Margaret the eldest, then four boys and me at the bottom of the pile – the runt of the litter. Mum was in her 40's when she had me, she frequently told me I was a menopause baby, not wanted, and she was disappointed I was a girl, not a great start!

We lived in Herne Hill in South East London – it wasn't such a sought after area at that time! We didn't have a bathroom, just a big tin bath hung on the back door, which was

filled on a Sunday night. Being the youngest, guess who was last in the water?! It wasn't bad though, I loved bath night! I can remember playing in the yard of the house, stirring up sludgy rainwater in an old bin – adding twigs and leaves to make a potion, it amazes me I can remember this so clearly, I was only 3 years old when we left that house to move into a brand new council flat in Charlton.

It was very exciting; we had an indoor bathroom and toilet! My sister Margaret was my main carer as mum was busy with the boys. I remember Margaret giving me a white teddy bear to hold when we were travelling to the new flat to comfort me.

One of my brothers, Richard, was very ill at this time, which is why we were lucky enough to be given the new council flat. It was becoming too much for Mum and Dad to care for him at home as well as the rest of us. A place had been found for him in the Goldie Leigh Hospital in Abbey Wood, a special hospital adapted for the care of children who were classed as 'mentally subnormal'.

I don't know the full details of Richards illness. The family story is that when Richard was six weeks old he contracted the chickenpox virus from one of the other boys which resulted in him developing encephalitis (inflammation of the brain) leading to frequent seizures and an inability to develop and progress in the normal way.

Clearly this put amassive strain on our family, I'd never known anything different, so to me it was normal. We would visit Richard in the hospital as a family, but as I was so young, I wasn't allowed into the hospital – I was told it was because my presence would upset all the children living there, so I had to wait outside in the garden, they would bring Richard to the window so I could see him.

I was six when Richard passed to spirit at the age of nine, he was still like that six week old baby. I wasn't allowed to go to the funeral, I was sent to school like it was just another day. This affected me for a very long time – a significant message of not being wanted. I'm sure they were good intentions, but nothing was explained to me, it was assumed I wouldn't notice what was going on.

I can remember taking one of my school friends to the corner of the playground on the day of the funeral, I asked her to stand with her hands in the prayer position. I said goodbye to Richard, thanked Jesus for his life and asked him to look after him from now on. My poor friend, she was very kind to go along with me, it must've been scary for her!

It is one of the hardest things in life – to lose a child – under any circumstances. My parents coped by closing down emotionally, I don't think my Mum ever got over it. Consequently, there was no expression of love in our family. No-one ever told anyone else they loved them, nor showed any loving behaviour towards one another.

Margaret, my sister, has always been very kind to me and as a six year old I adored her (I still do!), but she was building her own life, she'd left school, had a job and had met the love of her life, and together they were planning their future.

I desperately wanted to be loved, I had so much love to give! I found solace in books, so I knew how love should work. Somehow in all this, I assumed that I simply wasn't good enough to be loved. I developed a habit of telling lies – a great attention seeking device. Obviously I didn't know why I did it at the time but it's clear to me now looking back.

Margaret and her boyfriend Chris were married. One my happiest childhood memories is of being their bridesmaid. It felt amazing and I was honoured to be a part of their special day.

Then on my eighth birthday, Margaret gave me the most precious birthday gift – a new baby niece. It was so exciting to have a baby in the family and I loved her so much! Karen was a joy to have in the family, but this also meant that Margaret and Chris moved out of our family home to set up their own home. I would spend as much time as I could at their place. It was like I'd known Karen forever; we have always been very close.

One of my brothers used to scare me with stories of werewolves and demons coming to get me. He was to become attracted to the darker energies. Spirit was all around me, it was just a part of life.

I didn't always see, but always knew they were around. When my brothers had left home, I moved bedrooms.

The energy in the room was very unpleasant, I surrounded myself with light and asked Jesus and the angels to keep me safe. I would wake in the night to things flying around the room or my bedside drink being dripped onto my face. I could see the smoke from an old gas lamp on the ceiling above my bed – so many different things, but to me, it was normal. I didn't share this with anyone in case they thought I was quite mad!

As a teenager, I loved staying at friends' houses and learned that children were treated as valued members of the family, I soaked up that loving energy! Like all teenagers, my friends would moan about their parents or siblings, I always thought that what they had was amazing! I never took my friends home; I was ashamed of how we lived and treated each other.

I became part of a crowd in a pub near to my school, which was a long way from my home. It was all superficial, no meaningful relationships, but I liked being a part of this group. Some were pretty wild, and I loved the danger – I was underage and one of the youngest in the group.

It was quite a long journey home from the pub, I had to get two buses and if the timings were out, I'd miss the last bus and have a long walk. It was one such night that I was standing in Woolwich town centre hoping the last bus would arrive when I noticed a white transit van parked nearby. The male driver of the van kept whistling and asked me if I wanted a lift as I'd missed the last bus, which I declined. He drove away, much to my relief. However, he kept driving past the bus stop in each direction and I realised I was in danger.

I clearly heard a voice telling me to run to the street running parallel to the main road. I began counting how long the van would disappear from view in each direction, so I knew how long I had to run. I took my chance and ran to the dark street – I was afraid but completely calm as I had constant reassurance from the voice. It was the most loving, yet insistent voice!

The street I had been guided to was very dark and scary, but I was reassured I would be safe as long as I kept an eye out for the van - I was talking out loud to the voice all the way. As I reached the end of the street I had to cross another main road, I was told to wait, and I hid in a shop doorway as I saw the white van drive slowly along – he was looking for me.

Listening to the guidance I ran as fast as I could across the road and disappeared into a churchyard. Usually the last place I would want to be late at night, I was guided through to the other side and took all the quiet back streets until I safely reached home. It was Jesus who had guided me, I knew this intuitively, he has always been with me, particularly in times of stress or danger.

It didn't put me off going out or staying out late and I experienced at least two other occasions of being chased home late at night. I'm so grateful for the guidance and intuitive feelings warning me and keeping me alert. I didn't tell anyone about these incidents, I was ashamed that I'd told lies when I'd was younger,

I didn't think anyone would believe me, it would be just another of Julies' fantastic stories.

It's interesting that I safely survived all these events, but the one time I thought I would be safe turned out to be one of the most dangerous. A man I'd met a few times walking to work in Woolwich town centre asked me on a date. I was 16, it was my first job, with my own money and I felt very grown up. I agreed to meet him, he was going to take me into the West End, a new and exciting experience for me.

From the start of the evening it quickly turned into a nightmare. As we got onto the train, he had carefully planned for us to get into a single carriage – thankfully no longer in existence. He then forced me to perform a sex act upon him. I had no idea what he was doing or what I had to do – it was terrifying. We got off at London Bridge and we went into a bar, I was in shock and totally out of my depth.

He allowed me to visit the ladies, I didn't know what to do. A lady came into the toilet and I asked if she could help me, she looked at me like I was a piece of muck on her shoe and went into the cubicle ignoring me. I brushed myself down, tidied myself up as much as I could, took a deep breath and went back into the bar.

I honestly don't remember anything more about the evening until the journey home. I was praying all the way that I would be kept safe, I asked for Jesus to protect me once more. When we got back to Woolwich, he took me to the same churchyard that not long before had kept me hidden from danger, this time it kept him hidden from anyone seeing him rape me, he left me there in the mud.

I don't know how long I stayed there, I was numb, I had detached myself from my body and I wasn't ready to return. Somehow I got home, once more deciding not to tell anyone as I didn't think I would be believed, and I felt so stupid to have gone along on this 'date'. I never saw the man again. I put this experience into a box and buried it deep inside. It was many, many years before I finally acknowledged what had happened to me, I'd always believed it had all been my fault. This is the first time I have shared this experience.

After a few months I started going back to the pub, arranging to stay at friend's houses to avoid the long, lonely journey home. Everyone began to pair up in the group, so I started seeing Steve, he was quite nice to me and it was another step to fit into this group – he was six years my senior – I was 16 he was 22. I met his family and his mum used to make such a fuss of me! I thought – at last, a family I can fit into! Silly me!

I never loved Steve, but I liked being a part of something that felt safe. We planned our wedding despite knowing I didn't love him. I even called the wedding off 3 weeks before the date. Everyone went mental, my Mum told me I was selfish and how I was letting everyone down, the main feeling I remember from that time is loneliness. No-one asked what was going on, I was just 18 and easily cajoled into 'doing the right thing'.

So, we were married, and everyone enjoyed themselves. I can remember going into the toilet, shutting the door and saying out loud "you've really gone and done it this time". I had gone along with it to make everyone else happy – quite extreme lengths to go to just to try and fit in. Also, in the back of my mind I thought if I had a baby of my own I would finally have someone who would love me for who I am.

Within a year, that baby would come along, we had our own flat and I loved it, creating my own home. Margaret was great, she gave me loads of advice and helped me so much in those early days of motherhood. Having Jenni was the most amazing thing. It was scary and I knew my life had changed forever and that she would always come first.

Being a mum gave me the fight I'd never had for myself. I didn't want to see Steve's friends and family all the time. They were all telling me how I should be doing things. I wanted them all to leave me alone to find my own way, it felt like they didn't trust me to know how to look after her, they all knew better and I wasn't good enough.

Life with Steve wasn't terrible but was pretty dull. He carried on living like a single man, going to the pub with his mates most of the time. Once again, I didn't seem to fit, except on my own with my baby. When Jenni was two Steve and I separated. He went back to live with his Mum, and I felt incredibly guilty for never loving him.

He had got into debt without me knowing, playing golf and

spending money on drink instead of paying the rent or bills. I went along to the council to explain the situation and thankfully they agreed to arrange a payment plan, so I could pay the rent along with the debt he had left me with. It was an incredibly hard time, but I began to learn a lot about myself. After we'd split, there was a lot of fall-out from both families, my Mum told me that I'd made my bed and `I should lie in it'. My parents didn't talk to me for about 3 months.

I had a lot of time on my own, I decided to go vegetarian as I became more and more aware of cruelty to animals and how I could, with a bit of re-education learn to eat without meat or fish. Probably one of my first steps in deciding how to live life the way I wanted to. Both families thought I'd gone completely loopy. I didn't have any friends; all my so-called friends were actually Steve's' friends and I was quite happy to leave them behind.

When Jenni was with her Dad, I started going out with one of my brothers and began to make new friends. They were bikers, some hells angels, again I loved the danger, it was exciting to mix with people who were all kinds of outcasts, they just accepted me as another weirdo in their group! I really had a good time and looked forward to socialising every now and then.

I had a hedonistic few months although there were never any drugs involved, some people smoked weed, but I was never into it. I had a few partners, nothing serious, I was just having fun, it was very empowering. No longer did I crave someone to love me and the strange thing is all the men I met wanted a relationship, I didn't, I was just having a great time! When you stop looking for something it turns up in abundance!

I was very careful to keep Jenni away from my new social life, which only lasted about 6 months. I had begun to like myself for the first time. I was doing ok as a mum and although my friends were never going to be lifelong, we enjoyed each other's company. I wasn't perfect, I wasn't clever, but I was having quite a nice time relying on no-one except myself. I'd had an important emotional break from my family, I wasn't a useless nuisance who was always in the way, I was a mum and I could be whoever I wanted to be!

Sadly, the old doubts and fears crept back. I had found a new state of independence, but money was tight, and I didn't know what the future would hold. After such a good period in my life, I slumped into the worst depression I've ever had, and it was difficult to pull myself out. I'd always been aware of spirit but had closed that part of myself off completely.

It's still hard to think about that time. I consider that I'm lucky to have had very few periods like this in my life, I know others have to deal with this a lot. There are times I could have slipped back to that place but have recognised it and managed to swerve it. It was like a dark vortex beneath me and I wanted to fall deep inside, but I was clinging to the edge.

I would lie on the floor all night tempted to fall in, it was only the thought of Jenni that stopped me, I had to keep going to look after her, I wasn't about to leave her. I can't tell you how I managed to come out of it, all I know is that it took time. I started to visit a Spiritualist Church in Eltham – without telling anyone. I wasn't sure if it was the right place for me, but it had the most beautiful energy and one of the very few places I could feel at peace.

Around this time, I had a smear test that had shown some dodgy cell growth. I was referred to a consultant for further tests. He wanted me to have a surgical procedure that I wasn't sure about. He treated me with disdain and contempt. He wouldn't make eye contact with me and when I asked questions he said it was none of my concern as I wouldn't understand his answers anyway.

My intuition was screaming at me to get out of the hospital as quickly as possible. The consultant told me that if I didn't have the procedure I wouldn't be able to have any more children. I refused the treatment and had to sign a disclaimer that if my health failed it was my own fault. I was afraid, I didn't know what to do next.

The universe stepped in and I found the most amazing lady who saved my life. I started seeing a homeopath for the physical trauma and gradually I began to deal with the dark emotional stuff too – I had no idea homeopathy could help in this way. Like many alternative therapies homeopathy treats the whole person, not just the symptoms (although they are a good indicator!).

She gave me the time and space to talk about things I never knew I wanted to talk about. She helped me to understand why I had the symptoms as I had never really dealt with my emotional baggage. She taught me to listen to my body, to my own thoughts and intuition and to believe in myself a bit more. It's a bloody tough road, but it is possible.

As Jenni was getting older I had more time to consider my future. I joined a teacher training programme to teach adults, it was great, and I loved it. I realised I had quite a creative talent and really wanted to help others. Once I started on this path, my aspirations increased. I was teaching local groups how to produce newssheets for their communities, then I applied for a job working and training in the media resources area of education.

Nothing is easy when you're a lone parent, juggling working and college hours, getting home in time to collect Jenni from school, relying on friends to take her in the mornings so I could get to work or college on time, cooking, cleaning, keeping her entertained – children's parties, school trips etc. etc. It was a hectic time, but I was really happy, finally doing something for myself.

This start in education turned into a 29 year career in secondary education – who knew?! I worked hard, was very committed to each school I worked in and gradually climbed the promotional ladder.

As I started my education career and training, I met my true soul mate and love of my life, Neale. He has definitely been my saving grace. He has always managed to bring me back from the brink of sinking into the dark again. He totally believes in me and loves me – for who I am – all of me. I have wondered why over the years but have learned to accept that he just does, and I know we make a great team!

Despite the prediction of the hospital consultant all those years before, and with the help of my homeopath, Neale and I were blessed with two gorgeous girls as sisters for Jenni. Sophie and Poppy completed our little family. Our three girls have brought us joy and laughter, a few tears and an abundance of love like you could never imagine.

I didn't need any more evidence that homeopathy works – I didn't need any painful, traumatic surgical procedures, I trusted the remedies. All the time the girls were growing up, I self-prescribed homeopathy for them, I picked up a little book to guide me and used my intuition to find the best remedies for their various childhood ailments.

I still went to the GP to get the diagnoses, then consulted my little book. When Sophie was 3, she developed eczema and my little book wasn't enough. The GP prescribed a hydrocortisone cream – which was horrendous – it made the eczema so much worse! I returned to the doctor and I was so angry – how dare he do this to my child! I told the GP that I was going to take her to a homeopath. His response astounded me!

He said his father had been a homeopath in India and that he could refer me to the Royal Homeopathic Hospital in London for Sophies' treatment – I had no idea it was available on the NHS!! This information is never forthcoming from the GP's, if I'd not told him my intention, this would never have happened.

After a few months treatment, Sophies eczema cleared up completely and she has never had a problem with it since – she is now 29! I'm so glad we were able to get that help for her at such a young age and prevent years of difficulty with this awful skin condition. Sadly, in recent years the government has decided to withdraw the availability of homeopathy on the NHS.

As our little family grew, we became good friends with a couple who had girls of similar age to Sophie and Poppy. We had a fantastic few years with these friends, we went on holiday together and spent lots of time in each other's company, we became very close and laughed an awful lot.

Sadly, their marriage was in difficulty and this had a massive impact on Neale and me. We felt such a sense of grief, seeing our good friends and their children go through this difficult process. The woman I'd thought to be a true friend, with whom I'd shared so much, changed beyond belief.

I felt such a desolate sense of betrayal, things we'd shared she twisted and made ugly, it was like she wanted to tear my relationship with Neale apart too. It was a very difficult period in our lives, but somehow we got through it and I'm so grateful that we did. We sold our house and moved a short distance away, this helped us to recover from the bombshell that had dropped into our lives.

My work at school continued to flourish, I was taking on more and more responsibility and loving it. My visits to Eltham Spiritualist Church were also becoming more and more frequent. I would arrange my meetings so I could leave school in time on a Wednesday afternoon to attend the service – and I didn't have to tell anyone where I was!

Gradually I was brave enough to tell Neale about my visits and even encouraged him to come along with me a couple of times. I started to read a lot more about spiritual stuff, I bought a Silver Birch book and it resonated with me so much. I attended a workshop day at the Spiritualist Church, I was so nervous, I didn't know anyone, but felt it was a step in the right direction. It was incredible!

A lot of stuff started to come up – which I quickly pushed back down – but I was able to give readings to people which were amazingly accurate – I could see things and smell things so clearly, I totally surprised myself! I knew I wanted to work with spirit, I just didn't know how.

To get away from our busy London lives, Neale and I would spend an occasional weekend in Broadstairs in Kent. It was the perfect get away and we fell in love with it – hook, line and sinker! One day, whilst sitting outside a delightful café, the owners of the B&B we were staying at walked past and gave us a wave as they made their way home. Neale suddenly said, "their day is done, they've walked their dog and are on their way home".

It was about 2pm. It was a bit of a lightbulb moment! So, we started to plan our escape to Broadstairs. We put a 4 year plan together that actually manifested within 18 months – it was clearly meant to be! I continued to work at a school in London whilst Neale started running the B&B. Everyone thought we were barking mad, we did wonder to be honest, but decided to be brave and go for it! It has been one of the best decisions we've ever made, we continue to be really happy living and working in beautiful Broadstairs.

At the point of leaving London I discovered reiki – or more accurately reiki found me! I had heard a little about it, but suddenly it kept popping up, articles in magazines, online posts, books that I would pick up. So, I found a reiki course in London and achieved my Level 1 attunement. It totally blew my mind, this is what I'd been looking for, it was incredible!

Suddenly the world looked brighter, I could see colours I'd not noticed before in plants and trees and around people. However, I'd not realised how open my own energy was, and I had a huge healing crisis. My joints swelled and I was unable to walk, I was off work for a month, which was totally unheard of for me.

The doctors had no idea what was happening. It was during this time I realised things had to change. I had become increasingly unhappy at school and so decided it was time to go. I took early retirement so I could spend more time with Neale running the B&B. Which also meant I had more time to spend learning reiki! Within a few years I had completed Usui Level 2 and Master/Teacher Levels.

I absolutely loved working with this energy. I was seeing a reiki practitioner myself and decided to repeat my Master/Teacher level with her as she taught a slightly different style of reiki –

Holy Fire Reiki. Again, I felt my energy increase as I adjusted to this higher vibration. I started seeing my own clients, including guests staying at our B&B.

In December 2017, I was invited to attend a Winter Solstice meditation in Ramsgate. As we arrived, a woman glowing and radiating love came towards us and gave me the biggest hug I think I've ever had, she was Tina Pavlou. I'd never met anyone like her, and she has been a major help in my spiritual development. Suddenly all the things I'd kept to myself, was totally normal in Tina's world – hoorah!

I'd met a group of women who knew what I was talking about, had experienced similar things and were so welcoming. I attended the Theta practitioner training course, and a lot of the deeply buried emotional stuff has finally been faced head on and I have another element in my spiritual toolkit! I also met another true friend at this time, another talented spiritual worker who has also helped and encouraged my spiritual education and development.

I still don't fit into this world, but I am at peace with that, I don't need to fit. I am unique. The most important place that I do fit is with Neale and our girls. On December 7th 2012 we were married, on the 25th anniversary of our meeting. We were surrounded by friends and family who love us, it was a very different experience to my first wedding!

It still sometimes surprises and hurts when others forget to work in the light, get distracted by life and allow their ego to take control. But mostly, I'm happy not to fit.

I am almost at the point of graduating as a fully qualified homeopath, a real blessing in my life. I'm so lucky to be able to share this gift with others after it has saved me from unnecessary trauma and illness. Homeopathy is an energy medicine, just like Reiki. My experience with Reiki and Theta fit together so well with homeopathy, and it fits with me too.

I know that I chose my family, I know I chose to be on the planet at this time. A time when the world is in turmoil and chaos is all around and yet the light is getting brighter. I am here to heal, to help others on their journey through this thing called life. I am here to teach, this world needs healers. We need to stand together in the light to raise the vibration of the planet to live in peace and love. I am here to learn, every day I learn something new and it's amazing!

I know that Margaret, Karen and I have been together in past lives. I know that me, Neale and my girls have shared lives before and will do so again. Precious friends I have met in this life have been a part of my journey before and I'm so lucky to have met and recognised them again in this life. I know I am a spirit in a human body.

I am grateful to the angels, archangels, guides and mentors, including Jesus and the beautiful Mary Magdalene who are with me every day.

I am thankful to all the teachers I have met in this life. Every experience I've had has taught me valuable things and have made me the person I am today; I am grateful to them all.

I am so excited to continue my work, to heal, to teach, I am not afraid to return home to spirit when the time is right.

I am being guided to work with women suffering with menopause symptoms, funny that I was a menopause baby – perhaps it was always my destiny? It is the time of a woman's life to be embraced, not delayed with chemicals or mocked because of the symptoms. The new energy has much to teach you and I am here to help you understand.

AUTHOR BIO

JULIE TAYLOR

Julie Taylor is an intuitive psychic, healer and aspiring home-opath. Trained as a Usui and KarunaTM Holy Fire Reiki Master Teacher, Theta practitioner and Weleda Well-Being Advisor, she lives and works in the seaside town of Broadstairs on the Kent coast.

Together with Neale, her husband and partner of 32 years, she owns and runs Copperfields Vegetarian Guesthouse, where she organises and hosts healing and well-being mini-retreats.

For most of her life, Julie would describe herself as being in the spiritual closet with the door firmly closed! Always aware of spirit, she was worried about what others might think and fearful of being 'seen', so she kept this part of her life very private.

Born in Dulwich as the youngest of six children, Julie grew up in and around South East London. For 29 years she worked in secondary education, 29 years of imposter syndrome.

She never felt complete, always striving for the next thing and constantly wondering how she'd managed to attain her various positions of responsibility!

These were not all unhappy years, but Julie always knew there was more for her to do to fulfil her life. When she left the safety of her career in education, she finally found the time and the courage to step out of that self-imposed closet.

Julie was introduced to Tina Pavlou when she attended a Winter Solstice meditation in December 2017. Not knowing what to expect from such an event, she was blown away by the welcome she received – this woman glowing with love whom she'd never met gave her one of the biggest and most meaningful hugs she'd ever had! It was a beautiful evening and Julie felt she had found members of her soul family.

Ever cautious, it took another 2 years before she was ready to learn the techniques of Theta healing and to dig deep into her own soul journey.

The proud mother of three beautiful, strong, independent daughters, she has stepped up to clear the ancestral line of repeated destructive patterns through Theta healing.

At the age of 57, Julie decided to return to education and is currently a student at the Centre for Homeopathic Education in London, looking forward to graduating in the Summer of 2020.

Energy medicine is what makes her heart sing, seeing the profound effects of reiki, theta and homeopathy on her clients and patients is one of the most rewarding things in her life.

The link between homeopathy and reiki was a lightbulb moment for Julie and she looks forward to spending many years continuing to learn and help other souls to fit in and live peacefully in this sometimes hard to understand world.

Contact:

Email: thehappyhealerbroadstairs@gmail.com or julie.taylor@weleda-advisor.co.uk

Website: www.thehappyhealerbroadstairs.co.uk

Facebook: The Happy Healer Broadstairs @thehappyhealer11

10

KARALYNE KALACHMAN

I was born out of love and, I believe, wholeness.

From the tender age of 3, I took it upon myself to look after and parent my mother and my brother. It is a memory that has no words and is difficult to describe.

I became a young carer with no support, living in a war zone - chaotic, dangerous, frightening, uncertain, having to hide, as well as being violently exposed. I was working hard daily, no time for play, picking up the pieces, dealing with the fits and vomit and cleaning up the mess.

I was the vault that stored all the denied thoughts and feelings no one could express. My mother's pain had turned to violence. I was the target. I always knew when a schizophrenic rage was brewing because her eyes would turn black.

Most of my childhood was spent enduring emotional, mental and sexual abuse. The worst was the neglect. Being starved of love and affection, not being noticed or attended to for basic needs. No care givers or guardians, only a few distant relatives. It left me with very low self-worth. I was mostly silent.

I was taken to a psychiatrist when I was 4 because I stopped talking. I remember them giving me some games to play. They said I had a very high IQ and all they told me was that I took on my mum's pain. I now realise I took on all of her rage and internalised all the violence, including my father's and my brother's. It explains some of it.

I had no father and an absent mother. It made me a bit different. 'Orphaned' children often are. I was exposed to a lot of strangers because my mum was not fit to parent, she was drug dependent and mentally unstable. What happened behind closed doors was never spoken about.

Social services were involved but kept at a distance. I had no bruises on the outside, no one saw, or chose to see, what I was going through. At home I was caught in a domestic violence relationship with an adult who took pleasure in gaining power by being cruel, malicious and hostile.

Not many people talk about monster mothers. It is crippling. Her constant humiliation and punishments chiselled away at me over the years and stripped me of my sense of self. She told me I was ugly, and I felt it - for a long time.

My first memory of sexual abuse started at 4. Then again at 7 with another person. My brother took an interest when I was around 11, maybe before that.

I lie there in the dark. Waiting. I'm so afraid. The handle turns and I tighten the covers. I know they won't protect me. Still I close my eyes and pray to something I'm not sure exists. I hear the swishing sound of his legs.

He sits down softly as if he cares. He does handle me gently. But I know this is not love. I feel so alone. I swallow the tears and keep still.

The gentle handling becomes more forceful and urgent. I am so numb I am already above my body. Gone. And yet in moments of stillness I hear my heart thud against my chest, draining the blood from my veins.

Maybe that's why I leave? When he is done, he quietly moves his body away. Still no sound, only the smell of flesh and breath. He strokes my breasts and leaves his hand on my heart for a moment. Locking the secret in, keeping it safe.

I had loved him before this. With all my heart. He was the only man in my life. There wasn't another blood relation close. There wasn't one in his life either. Maybe that's why? He must have been hurt. He fed me with pills and even bleach when I was 3 and 4 years old. I was hospitalized 3 times. They all treated it like a joke and laughed about it.

But me, when he came into my room, I actually thought he was going to kill me. Like he tried to then. It may have been innocent.

He may have only wished to annihilate or wipe me out, even just
for a day. It was confusing and terrifying. I can still feel it now.

I was too frightened to tell about my brother. The threat of death was enough to keep my mouth shut. One day the rage came. It was so strong it made him stop. Nothing was said. We split in that moment and went our separate ways. It was a huge loss. He had been the only person in my life I trusted.

A few months later, when I was 14, I was raped violently by a man down the road. It went on for what felt like hours. I managed to say no in the beginning, but he was forceful, and no wasn't enough.

I remember the look in his eyes, nothing was going to stop him from getting what he wanted. I never spoke a word about it until I was 40. I remember saying no and then shutting down. I couldn't keep him off me. I didn't struggle. I kept quiet, like I knew how.

I ran away from home. I couldn't stand to be there anymore. I had a fight and went off to live with my alcoholic friend. A pattern of promiscuous behaviour followed. Sadly, it wasn't the empowered kind. I found myself 'frozen' again. It was so cold.

My friend moved away, and somehow, I found a job and a place to live. It was a strange house, but I felt safe there. I liked working for an international company where I met people from all over the world. I learnt about different cultures and it gave me a taste for travel.

I met a man. He educated me and taught me to read and write. He was borderline alcoholic like my father (his birthday was the same day as my father's), and it didn't end well. I was feral and he was drowning his feelings in a bottle. He tried to contain me, but I was uncontainable.

He told me I was psychotic: I had been. We never talked about our families. I had no words then. We held each other together with a sticky glue. When he left, I broke down. I had loved him like the father I never had. Acute psychosis followed with a lethal concoction of drugs, the internal turmoil got worse and the dark thoughts in my mind grew like a virus.

Poison ivy seeping through my veins, gripping on to the monster, like it had found a new home.

I remember waking up in the hospital, with slight awareness of the siren and the stomach pumping, then losing my hearing for 3 days. The nurses were kind, the psychiatrist not so. They tried to section me. I tried to be sane. I ran away before they could give me the treatment I needed.

It kept happening. I kept running. It was violent. More hospitals jabbing shots to the body and more toxic ingestion to stuff it all down. Still no one was listening. Certified insane, hysteric, impulsive, volatile, compulsive, explosive. Keep moving. Keep numbing. Don't be still. Ah some progression!! There was, at least, some movement.

Psychosis propelled me to the 5th dimension. I was already familiar with it. Dissociation (feeling disconnected from yourself and the world around you) takes you there. I had experienced the in-between worlds. When I was small, it was just a feeling that something was there with me. I had never seen visions as a child, only senses.

A new gateway opened. The visions came. Some were gloomy and some were glorious. I was boundless and free. Having no boundaries is a double-edged sword. It left me vulnerable to violation, and at the same time it gave me a rare kind of creativity. I didn't know how to use it yet.

I escaped to London. To get an education. I was determined to do it. With no basics in grammar or schooling I attempted a Degree. I was so stressed out my hair started to fall out and I was less than 6 stone. No one in 'my family' noticed. The wall of denial and turning a blind eye ran thick in this family. I don't blame them. They were sick too. The psychosis came again. Suicidal and on the run, I broke again. More medics and drugs to block the seeping holes.

Shape shifting between the worlds I met some interesting characters. From spirit and the people 'they' sent me. I was astral travelling, meeting dead people, spirits lost and found, wise men and women, and being gifted with miraculous events, people and animals.

The animals were my greatest teachers, they taught me the universal language and what love was. I was still lost and didn't know how to ask for direction. It was painful and the emptiness, at times, was unbearable. I tried to formulate a normal life. There were moments. I travelled and lived with shamans (and met my share of charlatans). They taught me about the natural world and my connection with animals grew stronger.

In my early twenties I began working in social care with people with learning difficulties on a farm. They gave me hope in humanity and saved my life; I felt very akin to them. They were earth angels. It was the first sense of what I was being given. Even though I was still plagued with suicidal thoughts, it was their love that got me through. Unfortunately, I burnt out quickly because I wanted to give them so much in return. Their parents had abandoned them too and even though they loved me purely, they too were desperate for attention.

Another 'missed' miracle led me to the dance: Gabrielle Roth's 5 Rhythms. It is a shamanic practice. It was buzzing. People were on natural highs and I loved it. It was the first time I met the Divine in person. Being fully awake and fully aware, I mean. I had no words for God at the time.

I most certainly didn't believe in that old beardy Caucasian man in the sky. But I started to see it everywhere. In all the faces dancing around me. I got addicted immediately, it temporarily kept me off drugs and I took off to town, London was calling me again. The force was compelling. I left with nowhere to go, unprepared for my next head dive.

I met Gabrielle Roth once, she said I was missing the heart energy. Quite offended I asked her what she meant. She said a father's role is to strengthen the heart energy, giving the child confidence and a strong sense of self. When there is no father, the child lacks the ability to speak its truth. I instantly understood. Thankfully the dance helped me communicate my truth, I had yet to find my voice.

I found myself grieving the only family I had known. The kids on the farm. I loved them so much. I had hardly stopped to say goodbye. It was brutal. I couldn't handle it and ran again. Next stop, psychosis my old friend, followed by a black depression.

The day I went to jump off a bridge, a homeless woman on the street came up to me. She was insistent and wanted to tell me a story. She said she had money, lots of it, but had made a decision to live on the streets for a year, as she was lonely and wanted contact with 'real' people. I thought I was hallucinating.

She went on to tell me it wasn't my time and that even though I was being directed toward the darkness, there was a reason for it. I remember my body being blown inside out like a bubble. She scuttled off and looked me in the eye and said, "I see you teaching many. Many. Keep to the path, even when it feels wrong".

Another Shaman came. She was a Medicine Woman, a French Mother Goddess. She told me I was a dancer. I knew that too. She said I must free my spirit and surrender to the dance. I spent a few months being around her teachings, simply absorbing, watching the visions and trying to make sense of them. I went to the West End and found myself becoming a dancer.

I followed a group of Sannyasins (disciples of Osho). It was a beautiful ride. A South American Angel appeared. We went on a journey together and I ended up dancing in a Gentlemen's club. At first, I was afraid to take my clothes off but after a few fizzies it didn't seem to matter so much. I really did love dancing and another Angel appeared.

This one was a force to be reckoned with. She was an Enchantress Goddess and opened the gate for my descent into the underworld. There was also an ascension to the highest of heights. Seduced - intoxicated - addicted. Possibly in that order. How did it happen? I only stopped to ask myself after the 'Great Fall'.

I was a wandering star, steering by starlight. The star led me across a tight rope. I followed obediently. The pattern was so embedded. How was I to know? *'The road to hell is paved with good intention'*. The shaman was right I found my freedom. But at what cost? I was liberated. Little did I know I was binding myself back to the chains of the past. Before I knew it, I was back there.

At first, I worked hard, sweating the night away, constantly dancing on the stiletto of life. I couldn't do the verbal performance; soothing their egos, filling them with false hope and fuelling the fantasy of the private dancer. It wasn't me. I had the intelligence but not the will. I could use my body. I was good at that.

It was inherent and I did it with effortless grace. I stayed clean and kept on working from dusk 'til dawn, along with a day job, averaging around 2 hrs sleep a night. I met the most beautiful women. They were pure inspiration. Brave and fearless.

Broken. I was home. It wasn't just me alone anymore. I worked and worked until I burned. I lost my home, found a coach and sofa surfed for a while. I was chaotic enough, let alone trying to arrange beds for the night. I got locked out one night and that's when things started to go really wrong. It wasn't mean or intentional. It just was. I found shelter in the rain.

By now, I was taking a little something to keep me awake. The alcohol wasn't enough. The dysfunction took its grip once more and chaos followed. The circus was seductive, the theatrical performance, the hidden dungeons of the Fetish scene, going deeper into the underworld and deeper into the Shadow.

It was fascinating and familiar. In the beginning it opened doors to secret boundless worlds. I felt drawn to explore, like a wide-eyed child without parental guidance. The downfall was inevitable. This world gave me an amazing experiential psychological training ground.

My studies took on a life I felt privileged to see and be a part of. It all swirled so fast and soon I landed in the place I had begun. It was a natural evolution. Gentle persuasion and sly manipulation. It was never a conscious decision. I know that now. It took me a long time to understand. How easily I was led. It's not that I wasn't smart. I was. I just fell into doing what I had been trained to do from such an early age – obey and "serve" without question.

This is the hardest part to write, I have never spoken the words out loud and probably never will. There were some deeply beautiful moving moments, and moments of torture, some physical. I met some breath-taking souls and some intensely disturbed human beings. I wanted to understand, I was curious, and I felt something pulling me into the Shadow.

The psychosis flittered in and out, but I managed it well with handfuls of powders, liquids and pearls. Still homeless, I was following instructions. It didn't seem so bad at first. But the path became a split road between heaven and hell. At times it was sacred. Other times, it was violent. The drugs and alcohol took the edge off. One day I decided to straighten up and stop the drugs. Bad idea. Very bad. It was an awakening I was not ready for.

I found myself in a room full of men and a handful of working girls. I knew what I was doing there but, in truth, I did not know what I *had* been doing there. The sobriety of it shot me way beyond the 5th dimension. I signed up for most of it. I own my part and I know now I was not in a state *to make* a conscious decision. I watched what they were doing to my poor body. I cannot tell you exactly what happened on that sobering night. It was not the first time, but this time I felt it.

All of it. I could not extract myself from it. I was frozen. Back to that place I knew so well. Not moving, not making a sound, training my pain to stay silent. I woke up and realised every one of these women had travelled an acutely similar path. We were being bought and sold. Like we were when we were little. We were all dying for affection. In the wrong place. Not wanting to be there at all. Numbing ourselves and acting out a mutual past at the service of others. This is so painful to write. Something is moving me to tell the truth.

How did I turn my life around? I didn't do it all by myself. I did find my way out. I found a sanctuary. I was so worn out. It didn't stop. I was still drinking. Divine timing hadn't yet struck. The angels were there, doing their best to guide me. And SHE was there - The Magdalene in the Shadow, always by my side.

Towards the end I was shown a vision. It showed me how I had tied myself back to the past (I was tied up with gaffer tape in a chair) and only I could release and cut myself free from it. I was then taken to another dimension where a 'master' spoke to me and told me everything I wanted to know about how the universe worked. I knew the answers to everything I had ever wondered about.

It was lucid and real and then the 'master' told me I had a mission and it was time to prepare myself for it. Everything that had happened was 'all in order'. I couldn't quite decipher the last bit, but it was message enough. The 'master' appeared both male and female and became the source. It said, 'He is the seeker, and SHE is the Source'. I don't remember anything after that.

The saving grace came when my hands started to go numb. I went to write something down on a piece of paper and it looked like 3-year olds hand writing. I knew something was wrong. That day I was referred to the hospital for an emergency MRI scan. I was waiting outside, and the vision came again, it told me it was time to stop now, something was drawing me to another life.

I thought it meant I was going to die. I was relieved at the time and remember thinking, finally I can rest. Six weeks institutionalised in the hospital; I came out drugged up to the eyeballs on intravenous steroids. They thought I had had a stroke. I was later diagnosed with Multiple Sclerosis.

The white coats gave me many diagnoses from, Bi Polar Disorder; CPTSD; Cyclothymia; Psychosis, Social Anxiety Disorder; EID to Developmental Trauma. I wasn't in love with any of these labels or the suggestion that I was likely to find myself in a wheelchair in a few years' time. The MS was progressive; I had put on so much weight with the steroids, I lost the use of my right arm and couldn't even do up my buttons or chop up my own food.

The blackest depression came, the projection of the future wasn't good, I'd lost hope. I believed I deserved it and became victim to it. I had some therapy to plaster the wounds. It helped but the black hole didn't disappear. I knew I had to heal it. I had come too far.

Recovery began with a 12 Step programme. It was a fight. Especially with God. I did not believe in God and could not believe in *Him*. Sorry mate, not having it. I went in kicking and fighting, scratching and biting. But something made me stay. I was on my knees; I'd hit rock bottom and I knew it was life or death. Literally.

I went to a CA (Cocaine Anonymous) Convention in Brighton. I had already decided it wasn't for me. Then a woman named Amal got up and spoke. Something happened. The veil was lifted. I saw the Christ. I bloody saw it. There was no mistake. And then again outside when I was talking to her. It came again. I knew what it was, and I told her.

She looked back at me with tears streaming down her face. I will never forget that moment. The Universal Christ (Buddha, Krishna, ISIS, all of them) spoke through her. It didn't demand religion or dogma. It was pure. It was love. I had seen it before. This time clearer than ever. I have seen it since, a lot, now that the Awakening has happened. It took another 4 years to come.

I didn't say a word in the Step meetings for 2 years. Speaking in a group was terrifying. A person with no identity, I had acute anxiety. Chronic, constant angst, being out of my body, sweating profusely, and leaving puddles on the seat. It wasn't attractive.

Blood sweat and tears.

Writing those words is biblical. I was 'guided' and given the message I would 'be healed' by a woman I'd become close to. I was ecstatic thinking it was going to be something wonderful. It wasn't quite what I had anticipated. It turned out to be the most excruciating experience of my life. The words have just come to me; 'I was taken to the Christ'.

I literally, in this moment whilst I'm writing, just saw a vision of the crucifixion. It was my time to enter the Shadow, to take a look at myself so that I could look at others differently. It was an extended dark night of the soul. I cried every day for 2 years, I got off the drugs, boarded myself up in my house, said my prayers and dug deep, deeper than I thought humanly possible.

The pain cracked me open, physically, mentally, emotionally and spiritually. I thought I was going to die. I did. I was reborn. Not in the happy clappy way. Nope. In a "stripping my insides out back in and out again" kind of way. Looking into the darkest corners of my psyche. I was being led to the cross to hang and to see the world with new eyes. When the dawn broke, I saw the heaven on earth.

> When the Awakening happened, I realised they had always been there. Even in the darkness and all the loneliness. They never left. This time they showed themselves in real human form. They are born on earth and they too have struggled to find their mission.

> They were led. It took time for them to know it. When they did, they turned over their will and opened themselves up to the work of spirit. They did The Work and their souls were cleansed. Attuning them to the light. Redirecting them to the plan written only by the fine hand – true service.

Since entering the Recovery phase of my life, I recognise them immediately. They come in all shapes and sizes, ages, colours, genders, sexualities, they are sometimes called empaths, earth angels or light workers. We are all children of the Divine. Every one of us is, whatever you believe in. Gently being called by the Goddess to Awaken, Heal and bring us back to the Source of who we really are.

While I was healing, I went back to work in mental health, got my diplomas and qualified. I thought I needed pieces of paper to prove my then, 20 years of experience. I had hope. Even though I was still struggling alone, I was being guided and the more I developed faith, the more divine miracles entered my life.

My clients were brave and determined, they too became my teachers. I began The Work - the deep Shadow Work required to become a guide or teacher. I learnt I had been fixing on everything and anything I could that distracted me from re-attaching to myself – alcohol, cigarettes, powders, pills, liquids, sex, work, people, and love addictions. I couldn't help it then, I really couldn't.

It was such a forceful energy. I had to work my way through all the levels before I could stop. I believe the drugs and alcohol saved my life. It sounds like a funny thing to say. I simply could not manage what was going on inside my head and my body.

I loved my years of practice, I got to share the gift of psychosis with hundreds of outstanding children and adults, but I struggled with the clinical approach. The insistence of the permanent labels. Mental health is always Emotional health. There is always a root cause, which is what needs to be treated.

My understanding of the Mind is that it encompasses our whole being. We are not compartmentalised. In a clinical environment it was frustrating. It wore me down, I still felt alone and in the 'wrong world'. I had to take some time out for myself. It was a hard decision. I'd hardly taken any time off all in the years I'd worked there. I was exhausted.

I was offered a place in a Community, a full time 2-year programme with a group of 30 people including 8 therapists. It was the hardest thing I have ever done and the truest and most miraculous gift I could have ever imagined. I was with people who had held in the most horrific stories as long as I had.

Being raped by their parents as little ones, abandoned and sold to paedophile rings; groomed by carers, thrown into care and chronically misused, the stories went on and on. Every one of them was an earth Angel. The most dynamic ones I had met. 'The Terrapins' (therapists) were not ordinary human beings.

In a moment of extreme emotion, I saw their wings one day. I was lifted out of my body and floated above. They just sat there with their normal therapist expressions (funny) and, as I looked around the room, I saw that every person in the room had wings. Some of them were folded, still afraid to rise.

How joyous to be shown. How sad that these beautiful beings believed they were so wrong. My heart is elated as I think about each and every one of them. How deeply blessed I am and was, to share that journey with these precious children. The gift is in the wound. For all of us.

Throughout that time, I was able to find forgiveness for my family of origin, my abusers and rapist. I had tried before and thought I had cleared the past with spiritual practices.

True forgiveness comes only when it is Given to us to heal. I understood my mum's pain at another level and was able to claim my own anger – it was finally heard and healed. I learnt that their denial (my family's) of what was happening led to the psychosis - there is often one scapegoat in each family which makes that person the "mental one" and keeps them all trapped in the same cycle of abuse.

As I have healed, they have healed. They are still in denial, but I love them, like I always did, very much, this time safely mostly from a distance.

It wasn't until my mid-forties that I was able to believe I deserved to be loved (I had spent 20 years alone after being told I was a pervert for being gay). I had dreamed of love for a long time before I grasped the fact that I actually had to take action to change the belief that I was unlovable, including the patterns of rejection, abandonment and unfulfilling relationships.

The Work I did in Recovery and the Community led me to the Love of my Life. I was given a "message" I would meet Her on the dancefloor. I forgot all about it. At the time I wasn't looking. I wasn't ready for Her to begin with. Before I met Her, a friend mentioned her name and my soul knew instantly. I forgot about that too.

A year later, in October, another friend told me I would meet someone around New year. I didn't pay much attention. It happened on New Year's Eve; the Goddesses were awakened!

The Shaman was right I did find my salvation and my liberation on the dance floor - my Angel, my wife.

We work together now. She is a Relationship Expert. How funny. She is incredible. Relationship work is worth investing in, let me tell you. It has become the most important thing in my life. My wife and I also *work* (and play) at our relationship.

We accept responsibility for our daily experiences by practicing authentic communication and forgiveness, we go to couple's therapy when we need it (we do) and we have both learnt how essential it is to negotiate with loving connection – speaking with love and responding with generosity. We get hurt and angry, but we are learning new ways to listen and to cherish each other.

Don't get me wrong, I slip back on a regular basis, but I have gone from surviving to thriving. I made a commitment to heal myself with the belief I could do it, encouraged by spirit and the angels that came into my life. I did it and am now almost pain free. The anxiety is hardly noticeable, the IBS is completely gone, and I am not attached to any of the diagnoses I have been given.

Now I am committed to helping others do The Work and heal for life. It is simple work – clearing old outdated "stuff" to completely balance and re-align the body mind spirit energy in order to create a truly fulfilling life worth living without constraint or sacrifice. It is possible, for anyone. All you need to be is Honest, Open and Willing. I put my 30 years of experience into this work (personal and professional) and I see the results.

Every person and group I see feeds my inspiration. I am still learning and making mistakes, I always will be. I have been the lowest of the low. I simply *cannot* judge another person. I'm not saying I don't have moments, but my perception has shifted to fair exchange and balance in all things. 'Everything that is done to me I have done to another'. It may not appear so as things can be different but the same energetically speaking.

My personal survival guide consists of being around and communicating with animals; being in nature; the dance (making it a practice to drop out of my head and into my heart), consistent simple daily practice, regular (un-intrusive) touch, asking for help, early intervention (particularly in relationships), practicing forgiveness and acceptance, letting people and things go, continuously learning and owning my part in things, being a part of a community (this is forever shifting), and most of all belief.

I have 'adopted' three children along the way and I hope that I can continue to guide them and instil belief in them. Belief in miracles, belief in themselves and others, and a belief in the life-force that guides us.

> "This plan that has been made for us is not one of deprivation, it is one of fullness, joy and abundance"
> **Melody Beattie**

It is our birth right.

I am so glad to be given this opportunity to write about it. When I saw the title of the first book, 'When the Goddess Calls', I knew

SHE was back. The Magdalene was beckoning. It moved me straight away. I read it in awe and wonder. Every woman has a story to tell.

Read them, read them all, and be inspired to write your own. You will need an inspired woman to get you off your backside and get down and write it. Tina Pavlou is that woman. I met her and knew her straight away.

She is a truly wonderful being and teacher and she is completely genuine and egoless-ly generous. "Does it get any better than this?"

.

AUTHOR BIO

KARALYNE KALACHMAN

 *Karalyne Kalachman is an inspirational teacher in Personal and Relational Empowerment and she is a Behaviour Change Expert, specialising in Anxiety, Addictions and Emotional Difficulties.*

Her background is in Social Care Work, Teaching, Mental Health and Art Therapies. Since 2009 she has worked as a Behaviour Change Practitioner for the NHS and Community Mental Health Teams, as well as teaching Personal Development courses.

She has 30 years of experience working with vulnerable adults and people from a diverse range of backgrounds. She is highly empathic and has been on an incredible journey through life herself.

With an acute understanding of adversity, Karalyne has worked with people from all round the world to help them re-balance their lives, clearing patterns and behaviours that no longer serve them, thus enabling them to become everything that they are capable of becoming, and reach their full potential as human beings.

Her focus is on Self-Empowerment - teaching you how to balance and re-align your full potential, and on Relational Empowerment - discovering new ways to get the best out of your relationships. She shares her expertise in Relationship Skills with safety and respect.

Mind Management delivers training programs for individuals, groups and couples.

Karalyne has trained with Shamanic, Tantric and Angelic Healers in the UK, Americas, Asia, North Africa and Europe, including Tina Pavlou.

She is a warm and friendly healer of animals and people with a simple and grounded approach.

Her vision is to build a few loving homes for a loving family (with two and four legged wonders), including healing retreats and educational centres for ALL to Recover, Restore, and Re-balance, with bountiful playing and creative learning.

Her code word is Humility.

Her email address is: mindmangementuk@gmail.com

www.mindmanagementexpert.com

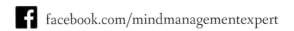 facebook.com/mindmanagementexpert

11

KYLIE SAVAGE

I was born and raised in a small coastal town on the Far South Coast of New South Wales called Merimbula, Australia.

The beauty of Merimbula is second to none as it showcases nature at its finest with pristine beaches, untouched bushland, and the all-round inspirational glory it offers.

My mum and dad are really hard-working family orientated people.

I undoubtedly know that this is where my integrity and compassion for others comes from.

Growing up I thought I was just a kid with a normal life. No signs of a gift, no extraordinary events just a shy country kid from a small seaside town.

It's only since I've been on this spiritual path that mum has started talking about the stories of when I was young and how every morning I'd tell her what country I'd visited and who the people were that I talked to, I could describe it all with vivid details which we now know would have been my astral traveling adventures but at the time not knowing any different my mum just thought I had a wild imagination.

I would also tell her about the girl in the white night gown with gorgeous flowing blonde hair, the girl I would play with every night, she would tap on my window and we'd play outside with the draught horses. So, I know now my gift of mediumship has always been with me in this life. However, it wasn't until I experienced the following defining moment that my real spiritual journey began.

I remember this moment so clearly. I was 24 sitting in my childhood bedroom, with all of my teenage posters still on the wall but now I had the addition of two little cots for my daughter Taylor aged 2 and my 1 year old son Noah. I had just left a violent and toxic marriage and I was so used to having to ask permission to do everything but all of a sudden this had changed, and it was now up to me to raise my children and discover who I was.

I remember thinking 'How the hell did I get here and who the hell am I! If I am no longer an army wife, and if I wasn't a mum who would I be? The answer was easy I'm Kylie'.

But it was in this moment that even my name sounded foreign to me, I had no idea who I was or what I should do with my life. 'Maybe the psychic in Townsville was right.'

I'd been to see a psychic in September 1999 and my mission was to get guidance to see if I should leave my marriage (because all life changing decisions should be made with the guidance of a total stranger with a gift right!)

The psychic was running late but I knew I couldn't leave. Despite the knots in my stomach I needed to know what I should do! My family had no idea of what was happening in my marriage because I couldn't tell them, I just felt so much shame. Finally, she arrived. We sat down and she shuffled her cards

"What would you like to know Love?"

"I'd like to know if I should leave my marriage?"

She started to laugh, "I'm not going to tell you that Honey. What I will tell you is that one of you has to be the adult in this relationship and that's going to be you!"

I hung my head in shame and fear, she grabbed my hand and said

"What I will also tell you is that you have *the gift* and within 18 months you'll be doing what I do."

My response was 'Lady, you are bat shit crazy! I would never do this work I'm not special enough to have The Gift."

Two months later in November 1999 I somehow found the strength to leave the marriage, a strength that came from wanting my children to have a safer, calmer, happier environment.

I didn't think enough of myself to leave. Now Fast forward back to my childhood bedroom in January 2000 and there I was with the realisation that I had no idea who I was or what my purpose would be, I didn't even know what I liked and what I didn't.

So, the search began to find out who the hell Kylie Savage is and if she is gifted.

I enrolled in every course I could. Meditation, chakra's, mandalas, past life regression even how to draw your guides. I read every spiritual book I could get my hands on, I was like a spiritual sponge and I wanted to know EVERYTHING.

One Saturday night my gift kicked in. I had three of the girls around for a get together where we would play with the angel cards. We would ask questions and get answers for ourselves by reading the booklet that came with the cards.

"Kyles don't use the book see what you get," one of them said.

So, I sat quietly and allowed the information to flow into me, the words that came out of my me were not my own. The information that was coming through was information I could not have known. In the coming months everything came to pass including the gender and birthday of my pregnant friends' child, this came from the information that I was relaying that night. It was the first of thousands of Channellings I've done since, yet I can remember that feeling of Creator flowing through me as if it was last night.

At that time of my life it was trial and error. I was learning how my gift worked and what I needed to do to get the best result for those I was reading for.

It was also at this time my mediumship became very strong as well. Every night I was crossing lost souls over due to the fact I lived across the road from the local pub.

I was constantly woken up by loved ones on the other side that just wanted to talk about their families, their life and the story of their passing.

It was through these conversations and asking a lot of questions that I got to experience and know the other side. You may call it heaven or the 4th plane of existence. I soon learned there was nothing to fear there and like my client's earth side these beautiful souls who had crossed only wanted to be heard and sometimes healed.

I see them as no different to working with a physical client and I offer the same amount of respect. Building these relationships so early in my journey is the reason I believe that mediumship now comes with such ease to me, I'm extremely comfortable with it. I also know how much joy it brings to my clients and their loved ones to still be able to connect.

After the constant sleepless nights feeling tired and worn out, I said to the Universe, "I'll do whatever work you need me to, but I have one condition. If I am to do Soul work at night my physical body must be allowed to rest, otherwise I can't continue to serve in the way that I do now."

From that moment I wasn't woken again unless it was an emergency.

Growing up, my faith was strong. I was raised as a catholic, heavily influenced by my gorgeous nana who was my heart, my soul mate. She was a women of immense faith and her belief in God was unwavering, she received the most amount of joy, preparing our local church for mass and my sister and I were always right by her side helping and listening to her stories about God and Mary.

To me they felt like family members that you could tell anything to so the biggest blessing I got from this time was my continuous conversation with God. I eventually stepped away from the catholic church no longer feeling in alignment with their teachings. I did feel tremendous guilt over this decision but mostly because of my nana and her connection to the church.

Nana passed away in June 1993 and I still feel the void in my heart. At times even though I can talk to her in spirit it's not the same as a big warm loving hug. This was an extremely confusing time for me as my gift continued to strengthen and expand and I asked a lot of questions because I had no one else to rely on but at the same time I also didn't feel I could talk to God, so I shifted my questions and aimed them to the Universe. It was at this time in my life that I decided to energetically call in my first teacher.

When the student is ready the teacher will appear....

In 2002 when I was 27 my teacher arrived in the form of a powerful New Zealand Lady called Su Sweetapple better known as White Bear. She had a gift like I'd never experienced before. The clarity of her channelling was mind blowing, her ability to heal others was limitless and part of her training was with the Hopi Indians. So, my training began in shamanism and ceremony and along came my introduction to Creator.

My training and adventures with Su lasted 9 years and took us on many medicine quests around Canada and the USA.

2005 was the year we would venture to Canada for my very 1st medicine quest and boy was it a massive learning curve for me. I came to learn the medicine ways from Cree and Inuit Elders and in true medicine quest fashion I was put on the pathway of amazing healers and teachers from all different backgrounds who would go onto be major influences in the way that I interpret Universal energy now.

It took a long time for me to process and see the bigger picture of this medicine quest and it truly is still the gift that keeps on giving.

I was so blessed to witness miraculous healings and have experiences that can only be described as impossible in our realm of existence, yet here I was right in the middle of these extraordinary events, being the witness and the record keeper to it all.

When I returned home life looked very different, maybe it was that I was different after all of my experiences in Canada. It was at this time I started dating my now husband Dan we had been good friends for the longest time and all of a sudden, we both seemed to look at each other differently, he understood who I was he'd walked a lot of my journey by my side already as a friend and knew that spirituality was something I did, it was who I was. I now had the support of a partner that I truly desired.

My spiritual growth was rapid with White Bear, she challenged me and encouraged me to find my own answers, which, at time was met with resistance from me because I was impatient, and I just needed to know right now! Looking back now I see that teaching me in this way I was empowered in my own gift and it strengthened my relationship with Creator connecting me to all that is and knowing that it's the only source we ever need.

In 2008 I had a calling to learn hot stone massage I shared this with Su so we started researching where we could learn this new modality. To our surprise there was a Santé Dakota Siox Medicine Woman coming to Sydney to teach traditional stone medicine which is also known as Geothermal therapy, the use of hot and cold stones on the body.

This is where my beautiful Mumma Bear enters my journey, Jenny Rae whose medicine name is also White Bear! Su and I took the medicine name as a sign. We enrolled immediately and booked our road trip to Sydney.

To our surprise we were the only students as well as the host, looking back now this was definitely one of those divine time moments. Being the apprentice of Su I took a back seat with my interaction with Jenny out of respect for my teacher, but I could feel the stones. It was like the stones were talking to me, guiding me, showing me how to dance them on the body, I was in love.

I'd found my spiritual family in the form of stone medicine. As we were saying goodbye to Jenny, I felt a really deep sorrow within my soul like when you say goodbye to your mum I couldn't contain the tears, she held me close and said "don't worry little one I'll see you in 3 months."

"Are you coming back I asked?"

She said, "No you'll be coming to visit me this time."

I couldn't wrap my mind around this. How would it be possible for me, a white country girl from Australia to travel and to learn with this powerful Medicine Woman.

It was 3 months later I got the invitation to travel to the states to learn more stone medicine. I cannot even describe in words what an honour this was; sisters from all over the world were invited to this retreat and I was one of them! This medicine quest to the USA was one of the most powerful events in my life, not only did I learn the traditions, but I learned who I was, I had completed my initial mission. I was here for my own medicine name.

The vision came in a very unexpected way and I say unexpected because I hadn't called upon it. I was simply experiencing a traditional treatment called 'Rainbath', a combination of hot and cold stones and Young Living essential oils. My healer was Janelle and even her name makes me smile. This amazing Lakota Medicine Woman has a laugh that would power a hundred cities.

We also share the same birthday, so I felt a deep heart connection with her. She began the treatment and as soon a she put the oils on I could feel myself leaving my body I remember saying in my mind "Creator what is this?" and all I heard was "It's your vision quest."

Now normally for a traditional vision quest you would be on a sacred mountain praying and fasting till the vision to your question is clear. Because of my faith in Creator I just went with it and knew I was safe. All of a sudden, I was a seal. A seal, swimming around all the oceans of the world I was told what my mission was for this life. A lot of my mission came through to me in story and so it took time to see the clarity in the story of life. I continue to choose to keep that whole experience in its entirety to myself because of how sacred it was.

When the treatment was over I could not stop crying. It was like a release I couldn't breathe or talk. I was overwhelmed by what I had just experienced. I shared as much as I could with Janelle between sobs, as she held me, she spoke softly to me and said, "So what medicine name did they gift you?" With tears still running down my face I answered, "White Seal Woman." Even after this life changing powerful moment with Creator and the ancestors, I still felt the need to check with Mumma Bear aka Jenny Rae if this was the right name, because I was after all still that country girl from Australia.

I went to the tipi to sit with Mumma Bear I told her the whole story the vision what had been told to me and my medicine name. She looked at me thoughtfully "This name was given to you by Creator and the ancestors little one it's the most blessed gift you can receive so yes your medicine name is what you were gifted." Of course, I cried some more, feeling exhausted and empowered all at the same time.

On my return home Dan and I decided it was time to expand our family and in December 2009 we welcomed our son Logan into the world.

In 2010 Jenny Rae came back to Australia hosted by Su to hold classes and ceremony.

It wasn't long after this that my apprenticeship with Su was complete and she moved back to New Zealand with her beautiful family.

Sadly, our beautiful Su transitioned across the river on 25 October 2016.

In true Suez fashion she visited me shortly afterwards to make me promise to look after her daughters' spiritual needs and healings should they reach out. She is with me often in spirit and I am forever grateful for the teachings and lessons that were gifted to me during our time on our journey together.

The last time I was with Jenny and Janelle was 2011 just before the Mayan calendar ended I was privileged to learn what this meant for the world and what my part was to help shift the old energy and allow the new vibration to begin.

These 3 Divine Medicine Women have been a massive part of

my growth and knowledge and without them I truly believe I wouldn't be doing what I am.

So, I honour each of them for the part they played in my journey.

My next turning point was in 2013 when I was pregnant with my 4th child. I felt like I was stepping into a new chapter of my life and I remember asking myself "If all I had was my gift and my way of doing things, what would that look like?" This was the start of some very deep discovery about myself because you see I'd had teachers instructing me since 2002 and now I was ready to soar on my own for a while. Time to discover what my intuitive recipe was and how to serve others in the best and highest way with it.

I stopped doing body work while I was pregnant and after the birth of my son Tanner, I really focused on the readings intuitive and mediumship. It was less physically draining whilst looking after my newborn baby. Not to mention, I was also working as a full time manager at this time, so I would do sessions on my days off or after work. I didn't do any other training at this time in my life, I was focused on my family and my work and I was totally at peace with this.

2015 was another massive 'Universe steps in and redirects you' event. I had changed jobs and this one was much more pressure; I was doing none of my medicine or spiritual work ....nothing. I was just in the corporate world with my head down and my bum up.

To be fair though, my guides had been trying to tell me I was heading for a crash, but I chose to ignore them because I was too "busy." The crash came on a Wednesday morning walking into work when I had a massive panic attack, I truly thought I was dying I could see the light I was going towards it and I was telling myself that this was it!

Then I heard "Are you listening now! You're not dying, it's a panic attack and a nervous breakdown. We are here." It was my guides still there loving and supporting me even though I'd been ignoring them for months. The love I felt at that moment was divine, I knew I'd be alright, but I also knew that I had to make a change.

The next month was a complete blur of Valium and Drs visits and the confrontation that came from my employer at the time. I was in a dark hole and one day rolled into the next, until one day when I was laying on the couch, bombed out on Valium I started looking at how this was affecting my husband and my 4 children. I realised that I was letting them all down, that this was not a life they deserved and that I was a mum that was not present for them. They were having to be the carers instead of me being the carer for them.

I looked up and said, "Creator this is not my F-ing life I refuse to live like this. Please, you have to help me."

I heard "look at your phone"

I opened up my phone and there on Facebook was a lady talking about branding yourself online making money from just being you and spreading your message it was like I'd been answered.

The course was $1000 USD how am I going to come up with that I'm not working I thought.

I walked into the kitchen where my son Noah was making a coffee

"What's good mum?" he asked, "I was just looking at this course honey but it's a bit out there for me just yet." He asked me all about it, why I thought it would be amazing and I told him, it would allow me to work from home till I recovered. His response was "I'll pay for it, if you believe in it, I believe in you. I started to cry "No mate it's fine you're only on an apprentice wage." He said, "mum I'll pay for it because I love you and everything you earn under the name Kylie Savage, I own 10%!"

That of course made me laugh he is defiantly an entrepreneur he makes me so proud as a mum, with his massive heart and his business mind. So, thanks to my son Noah, my journey as a spiritual entrepreneur began that day.

2016 was the year my online business began. It was also the year I was introduced to Theta healing™. I was focused on my business connecting with as many beautiful souls as I could, I had also decided that I didn't need any more courses I was at the peak of what I did intuitively. My good friend Zoe was a Theta healer and instructor and we would joke about doing swaps, but I really didn't understand what she did. We were at a business meeting one morning and I just heard "you need to have a session with Zoe today."

"Zoe, I need a session please." She almost fell off the chair, "OK let's do it today before you change your mind!"

Once again, my life was changed forever that day in what I can only describe as a miraculous healing. I enrolled straight away for Basic DNA, Advanced and Game of life, all within a 3-week span. What previously was taking me 7 to 21 days of healing for each client in a traditional manner was now taking minutes. I was hooked! Every Theta healing™ Course that was available I signed up for, with each course I healed more and more of my own wounds and cleared limiting beliefs and programs.

One day I was driving into town and I was talking to Creator, asking how I could reach more people and create a massive positive ripple effect to the world and what I heard was. "What about Facebook live?" Interesting, I thought. I'm not sure if I can actually channel online but it's worth a try so within 7 days, I had a new Facebook page called Connect with K so I could channel online.

I let all my clients know what I was doing and let them know I was having a trial run. That night I tuned in to Creator, I was getting ready to go live and there they all were, everyone's loved ones, waiting to connect with my clients on a Facebook live stream.

That night was the first of many live streams I've done since, I've connected for beautiful souls all over the world and I feel so blessed for that simple message from Creator.

It was also through the Live Streams that I decided to design my own Intuitive Development courses to teach others how to empower themselves through their own intuition and connection, I never wanted to be a crutch for people to lean on or rely on for guidance, instead I chose to empower them through knowledge, so they could make their own informed decisions.

In November 2018 I met the divine Tina Pavlou in Melbourne whilst she was teaching Theta healing™ courses. I'd been a Theta healing™ practitioner for almost 3 years and I was still attending every course I was able to. I had no idea at the time what an impact these courses and meeting Tina would have on me.

My first healing with Tina in this course was so powerful I just felt an immediate connection to her and shifted a deep wound I'd been working on most of my healing journey, the next 4 days blew my mind I had no idea how much could be healed in 4 short days. It was in the Divine Time meditation that I was simply shown a Zoom call with Tina, Joanne and Nicole and I felt the connection.

Two weeks later I picked Nicole up from the airport one of the first things she asked me was if I would assist Tina, Jo and herself at their Embody the Goddess Retreat in Bali the following November I knew immediately this is the vision I'd seen in my Divine Timing meditation, so my answer was "Yes."

At the time of writing this I'm currently counting down till November to be able to work with these divine ladies and make a massive difference to the lives of all the beautiful ladies attending.

January 2019, I felt the call to do my Theta healing™ Instructors training for Basic DNA , Advanced and Dig Deeper on the Gold Coast QLD this would mean my students could graduate to be a practitioner with all three courses. I've received so many blessings from this modality that I wanted to share that with as many students as possible. Watching that aha moment when they shift a belief or a trauma that's been holding them back for years is the best feeling.

As I look back over the past 20 years at all the challenges and blessings on this spiritual path I'm so grateful for it all. Every moment, the good and the bad. There has been plenty of heart ache, fear and trauma along the way, it's through our own personal healing journey that we gather the skill, compassion and awareness to then help others. The saying, "You have to walk it to talk it," completely rings true for my life and is the very reason I can facilitate the healing I do.

I know with everything in me I'm exactly where I'm meant to be on this journey. It is not to be rushed through at warp speed it's about taking the time to enjoy the moment.

We only have this breath, we can't re-breathe the last one and we can't pre-breathe the next one. So, in this breath be present and ask yourself, 'what I am choosing for me?'.

I am truly excited to continue on this spiritual journey embracing my Goddess energy and enhancing all the divine gifts I've collected along the way and will continue to collect.

I absolutely love doing my sessions in person but the magic of a phone session really light me up because they allow me to connect to people all over the world from my humble hometown of Merimbula.

I want each and everyone of you to know I am here for you, to support you, to facilitate healing and connection, all you have to do is reach out.

May the wind blow you many blessings

Kylie Savage xox

AUTHOR BIO

KYLIE SAVAGE

Kylie Savage lives in Merimbula NSW with her partner Dan and three of her four children. Her home is a place of love, laughter and end to end sessions with clients from across the globe.

Kylie has worked with thousands of men and women helping them connect to, clear and heal their Spirit for over two decades.

Extremely Fluent in the languages of the spirit world, Kylie is a world class powerful Psychic, Medium, Energy Healer, Medicine Woman, Channeler, Business Intuitive and Intuitive Coach.

Kylie has a unique ability to connect to the Spirit world and can download information on any subject, whether it's personal or business, then channel it to her clients via speaking or writing.

Kylie draws on a combination of clairaudience, clairvoyance, claircognizance, and clairsentience which allow her to hear, see, feel and KNOW energy and the Spirit that is communicating with her.

She can also often taste and smell whilst receiving messages for her clients, allowing her to understand the detailed messages she receives from Spirits and from Universal energy.

As a gifted Medium, Kylie is able to connect with the other side and communicate with clients' loved ones who have passed by receiving healing messages, knowing how someone has passed, and what their thoughts were at the time.

Kylie has been trained in many different traditional ceremonies by native Elders.

In addition to her many other gifts, Kylie is also a Medical Intuitive, powerful shamanic energy healer and qualified Theta Healer® Instructor and Practitioner.

With a strong online presence and her thousands of followers and clients, She is passionate about helping others to become the best and most positive versions of themselves, and guiding them to understand themselves, and how energy works, on a deeper level, which in turn brings healing, joy, happiness and peace to every area of their lives and to all those around them.

Email~ whispersbyk@gmail.com

Website~ www.connectwithk.com

Facebook ~ @KylieSavageOfficial

Instagram @ConnectwithK

$\mathscr{M}$y awakening was not planned... it just happened. I simply went into it. I accept the Universe just decided it was time.

The catalyst of my spiritual awakening happened when my dear dad, who was one of those people who had a great zest for life, sadly announced he had Cancer. As a seemingly fit and healthy retired man he went to his Doctor's for a routine health check and flu jab and found out he had Cancer.

As an only child, walking with him through his battle with Cancer was an opportunity to simply face the whole natural phenomenon of life and death, and to pray which started to open up my spirituality.... And my prayers were answered as the Angels started to open doors to amazing experiences to brighten up my life and bring fun and laughter back in to what was to become a period of time facing more sad events which rolled in like one big wave one after another without any mercy over these past few years.

If anyone had told me about the sad events, which happened in super quick succession, I would have to face after his death, I would never had believed them. I have collected the t-shirts for lengthy Probate; downsizing mum and settling her down; acrimonious divorce after a long term marriage and selling the matrimonial home in addition to redundancy!

They just added to being an overseas gran with the blessing of a third grandchild being born in Australia who joined the other two grandchildren out there, thus making me an over sees distant shore gran (and in your hearts of hearts being an overseas gran is emotionally tough). My purse was stolen when I was in London and I lost a special commemorative Birthday bracelet.

I got pneumonia and had to recover from fractured ribs on a yoga retreat in India, plus I fractured my nose when loft ladders fell on it as I was clearing the loft in the former matrimonial home. I ended up being diagnosed with post-traumatic stress disorder from Domestic Violence Abuse and had to go on a 3 month course.

It was just a steady collection of one bad t-shirt after another, and somewhere in midst of this a glass or two dropped wrong and I thought about suicide one morning ... so I got the T-shirt for that one too ... except the Universe had other plans for me that did not involve anti-depressants or being on a Mental Health Care Plan.

It involved moving forward on my spiritual awaking. In fact, no one would ever give me any drugs! They said I was fine ....the reason I guess was because I was spiritually awakening and that force was in me and around me and I was developing. I was healing and opening out like a flower in the sun.

It seemed really strange, looking back and reflecting on all this trauma, that in all of this constant drama ...my spiritual awakening gently happened and I am really glad it did. It was that diamond in the dark events I was constantly dealing with back then.

One event that was to bring light was meeting Tina Pavlou through Yoga. Yoga is one of my practices that has been a part of my life for the last 10 years. If I can bend ..I cannot break. I love my time on the mat and my yoga teacher is amazing.

Yoga is not just done indoors but outside, and in all different countries too. I love it when you can feel the union between your body, spirit and mind and get to that perfect point of peace. It has been really useful to learn different breathing techniques and also to feel confident about listening to my body....as I have learnt not to take it for granted. It's a gift.

I met Tina when I went to a yoga retreat in Glastonbury near the start of all my troubles. It was small group, and we went to at an

Ashram. I had never been to an Ashram before. It was there that I learnt more about the Hare Krishna way of life and spirituality.

The movement is a branch of Hinduism. I loved the food as it is prepared with love as they believe they are cooking for the pleasure of God. They never sample the food, which is always made with fresh ingredients, as it must be offered as part of a ceremony to Krishna first. I loved the music and mantra's and the fire ceremony service.

This was where, as part of a ceremony, negative feelings were said and offered to the fire from the congregation and then positive feelings were offered. It was very powerful. We also birthed our drums at the Retreat and my drum which I made is called Bill and I love him too.

Another thing I loved was the garden, it was beautiful and there was a sense of peace that I needed to grow strong in. The thing I have learnt about dealing with drama ....is to take time out. Sit on your Yoga mat, go on a Retreat, the answers and the strength will come and with fun, friends and laughter. It was a fab time xxxx

And, somehow, I naturally drifted into Tina's orbit. She was holding Reiki shares in a spiritual church. This is where my spiritual awaking began to develop. I knew I had a natural gift for the Usui reiki. This is a form of healing promoted by a Japanese scholar called Mikao Usui.

I never really planned to go to the Reiki evenings. I always arrived late but seemed to just be passing the area but as soon as I walked in I could sense the pain and blockages. I was in pain and I could feel other's pain and I wanted to do something about it.......and so I did. I started to learn and to be open.

The best thing about this form of healing was in the share's, I could place my hands on the clientor in their aura, but I could also whilst at home place my hands on myself and heal the Chakras which were blocked. It really started to accelerate my healing process as I was self-healing.

Then I saw healers using the reiki pendulum to ascertain where the client needed to be unblocked. And, you guessed it..... one naturally came into my life unexpectedly bought for me in a crystal shop, after I naturally connected to it in the shop. It became my confidence tool that my Usui reiki healing was working.

By now, I could sense blockages. I knew where both mine and the clients pain was, the reiki pendant just confirmed this. My reiki pendant became my party trick..... when there were block-ages or the chakra is unhealthy, the pendulum will move in a direction, other than clockwise. It always worked.

Plus, I was connected to it, I could ask it simple Yes and No ques-tions I needed to know the answers to. It was amazing. I would asked "whether my name was Laura" and the pendant would swing one way. I asked "whether my name was Clive (I am making this name up) and the pendant held over my hand would swing the other way.

I asked it if I would ever drive a Lamborghini car and it was a definite NO. I felt connected to this pendant. When I went back to the Reiki shares I used it as a tool to test whether the negative energy I had cleared was gone, if the person seeking healing was clear.

I later learnt how to self test by standing still and asking if my name was Laura. As I connected...I would fall forward ...then I would ask if my name was Clive...and I would fall back. Connected now, I could ask the Universe questions and get Yes or No answers. It was amazing.

But, more amazement was to come. I went on a Yoga Retreat to Goa in India. I went into a rock shop in the small resort, my reiki pendulum was in my bra. At this stage Tina used to give us crystals to help us and we were encouraged to wear them in our bra's, and as the reiki pendulum at that time was my favorite tool for healing myself, it used to spend a lot of time there.

Anyway, in this random shop I spied another reiki pendulum. It came from the Himalaya's. I sat on the Lino of the shop and started to place it above my chakras. Then, I took my much loved Bourton-on-the-Water reiki pendent out and placed it above my chakra's. It moved in exactly the same ways. Just like in the first crystal shop, I soon got an audience. They were amazed too. And so, I bought the Himalayan reiki pendent and a healing stick which went with it as a backup. Armed with these, it was just fun to heal.

Once I accepted my gift of being able to heal myself and others, it just so happened that Tina started to offer Usui Reiki courses. Before I knew it, I was working to be a Master.

As I was going through these courses, I had to learn a very important lesson........to protect myself. This is really important. I started to learn to ask permission to come into the persons space who was seeking healing and when this was given I learnt to protect myself. This meant working with the Angels. I used to ask them to put a cloak of protection around me or to zip up and to send all negative energy back to the Earth and I also had to learn how to disconnect properly.

As I learnt and practiced these skills I seem to naturally drift into the next level Usui Reiki level and then onto Master level. It all happened as naturally as that and as simple as that. I liked being in Control, especially as at the same time the rest of my life was wildly out of control. I liked healing people and seeing them feel brighter and lighter. I liked clearing negative energy away.

As I was learning about Protection, and calling on Arc Angel Michael for his cloak of Protection, I was becoming closer to Angelic reiki. This was harder as you needed to be clearer so the angelic healing could be channeled through you. I had to spend time everyday clearing my chakras.

This was done every morning through breathing, clearing my chakras using the pendants, and somehow a pack of tarot cards had descended into my life and when I felt the moment I drew just one and it always resonated. I was also finding lots of feather's and seeing numbers like 11.11 a lot and every time I went on

Facebook I was resonating with the messages. I could feel the presence of Angels, especially at night. They seemed to like to wrap me up. Strange, but true.

And that was when the steps towards Angelic Reiki happened when the Angel's kept wrapping me up when I was at rest. I could feel them quickly protecting me wrapping me up and letting me rest.

It was then I felt I will do the basic Angelic Reiki. I did it but I knew it was going to take more time for me than the other ladies to progress as Usui Reiki was one of the few things I had control of and becoming a channel for Angelic healing took a year of my life, more personal clearing every day, more time to connect and when I finally put up my hand to say I am ready ... it just so happened in my busy life that the courses I needed to be a Master where available. The Universe had my back and I had to trust it.

So now I was Master in Usui and Angelic. I only practiced on myself or on people who came to the Reiki shares but something bigger was coming......Theta Healing. I was so ill when I went to my first Theta Basic. It was snowing. I had the start of pneumonia and was driven to the course by a friend in the snow. I sat there on a wing backed chair in a blanket and everything Tina was telling us all started to become very interesting.

In the practice sessions without knowing anything about these people I was able to instantly pick up in their aura parts of their lives they were carrying. I was shocked at how my third eye had opened. I was also becoming aware that blockages can be removed and they can be from a genetic, soul, historic level.

And as I was contemplating this, Tina led a Fairies and Dragons Retreat where we visited Avebury Stone Circle. It was Amazing. This is the feminine energy, whereas, later (not that I knew at the time), I would visit Stonehenge, which is the masculine energy.

The Avebury Stone Circles are one of the marvels of ancient Britain. It's a very large circle of stones and there is a village and a beautiful tree that we all sat under giving us shade in the intense heat of the summer sun and gave our gratitude's and hugs and photo fun....it was just fun, laughter and great times.

PS...I did not feel dragons ... but I think the fairies were around! It was them that introduced me, in a light and bright way, to the fact that I needed to face up to my shadow self and shadows that were coming around me. And so, naturally, I bought their set of tarot cards ....and low and behold, just like my other brighter set... they resonated. It was spookily accurate!

Then, life became super super busy and the matrimonial house I lived in had to be finally cleared and sold. I had done such a lot of healing in the house that although I had only a couple of weeks to leave I wanted the house be used for a course called Theta Dig Deeper. The Spiritual Church has been sold and so Tina needed somewhere to run the course.

It seemed the natural, it should be held there. It was there, packing during the course, I felt the energies people released ... just as I had done previously in the house. I felt very proud of myself and of the people who had successfully completed the Theta Dig Deeper course during a beautiful hot summer weekend. I was grateful that my wish that this house would be a place for others to heal was granted. And, that what I am moving onto now, being grateful....it's as important as protection.

Learning to be grateful is so important. Every day I did and still do my mantra's and then gave thanks for the things I was/am grateful for. I have rather upped my game on this one though because when I went on my last retreat to Kovalam, India I took 13 of my much loved crystals for each day I was there and threw them into the sea with an "I am grateful for" .... I have made a note to myself that I will do this on every retreat I go on, and I have continued this practice.

The Goddess Rooms were set up in my local area and I have a safe healing place to go to and I was drawn back into the spiritual life. Fun, laughter and adventure were once more around the corner. The Goddess Rooms are on an industrial park. They have a business feel but they are filled with spiritual people on their own journey's who are being helped through the different healing modalities that are offered. I have been surprised at the number of healing modalities.

Retreats are one such modality, and before I knew it I was on a wonderful retreat for my last birthday. This adventure in the warm September sun was to go back to Glastonbury, to the Ashram. In this retreat, the Goddess Girls (as I call them) went to Stonehenge at dawn and watched the sun rise through the Stones; driving back to the Ashram, there were hundreds of hot air balloons in the sky which made the privileged experience of Sunrise at Stonehenge even more magical.

We had amazing workshops and as usual climbed the Tor; and, Bill my drum went back to his birthplace and his lovely sound was heard in an impromptu drum session in the orchard on a warm summer night. Amazing. And I will write it again Amazing.

And yes, before I knew it..... I was doing Advanced Theta and Dig Deeper at the Goddess Rooms. These were tough courses and afterwards there were healing crises which I had to work through. I had learnt by this time that it was safe to feel sad, low or down and to let these feelings happen. I was safe within myself to let my body release them.

I actually had no idea what was being released but I knew it was good for me to make time to let go. These courses are not for the faint hearted; and you need recovery time after, as you learn and release what is holding you down. I learnt to do it by myself. I could self sooth. The Shadow Tarot cards, although were a big shock, were spookily accurate, in some way they prepared me for going through the darker feelings of Advanced Theta and Dig Deeper.

Which brings me onto Unicorns. I met my Unicorn, Petroyguiya, in my second Glastonbury Retreat in a Unicorn workshop and again in my third (last) Glastonbury Retreat. The meeting had been initiated in a prior workshop in the Spiritual Church, where

I have a most treasured crystal which was found and bathed where two rivers meet.

There are photographs of the energies of the Unicorns galloping around us Goddess Girls.... just like there are photographs of us on retreats on the Glastonbury Tor with orbs on or nearby us. I would find it hard to throw this crystal back into water with a note of gratitude as I loved those moments when I felt connected to my Unicorn. They are light energy.

Manifesting and Abundance ... well, one of the countries I always wanted to go to and explore was Israel. For year's I would sell things at Boot Fairs to put into my Holy Lands fund. To cut a long story short....it finally worked out that I went this year by myself and had fun, laughter and adventure. And, despite the odds.... it all worked out.

The reason was it was meant to be at that time....it's called trusting the universe, and I do. I felt very connected when I did the Via Dolorosa in Jerusalem, which are the steps of the Crucifixion the same steps that Jesus walked. The stations or stops show where he was tortured, sentenced, carried his cross, the crucifixion, his death, burial and ascension place.

And then I went by myself to Bali, on a spiritual yoga retreat, where Eat Love and Pray was filmed. I went to a spiritual man out there and he said that I would go back to a place and that regular meetings about spirituality would come into my life and they were important. And guess what! When I returned to the UK, the Goddess Rooms started to hold Red Tent monthly meetings, which of course I have attended. It is important to be with like spiritually minded people face to face in addition to the Facebook contact groups.

All through my healing I have swam in pools and seas in India, Bali and in England. I have become known as a Mermaid. And Bali was particularly important because I swam with the Turtles. This was super nice too and I am very grateful for that experience.

Recently, I have experienced forking which is a sound therapy and this is starting to open me up again. I was surprised that I opened like a flower to heal, when I had I closed after my trip to Bali. I healed finally in Bali. The forking session made me realise that I now don't need to be scared to remain open to the Universe who helped me so much to heal and to continue to work to remain open. And so my-self work continues.

If anyone had told me, when I was walking the walk with my dear dad through the battle of Cancer, that I would end up in a world of fun and laughter and magic.... I would never had believed them.

Joss sticks, Gong Baths, going on a yoga retreat and sleeping on your own bed that you had just sold to them; crystals in bras, reiki pendants, the amazing accuracy of tarot cards, the power of the lay lines in Glastonbury, the energies captured in photographs such as the orbs on the Tor in Glastonbury or the energy of the Unicorns, the power of mantra's, mindfulness courses, Drumming Circles, cleanses, Epsom salt baths, mindfulness, sensual being workshop, eating well (I am a vegetarian/pescatarian) and blessing food and drink - especially wine (mines white), loving water and cleanses, waking up and thinking grateful thoughts, making sure your thoughts are good, being open but also self-protecting, acknowledging the power of the full moon and cleansing crystals under its light and simply being open.

My future is amazing. I manifested it. I did a Dream Board in Australia in a spiritual workshop about how good it can be to be on your own and enjoy your own company with fun, laughter and adventures. I love my dream board. Do one .... you just sit down with a big collection of magazines and travel brochures and cut out pictures that you are drawn too and then stick them on a piece of paper. It's fun.

My spiritual awaking has been directed to myself and I seemed to drift into it as easily as water going down a plug hole. I find it all really interesting. I have written this at the eleventh hour, but I hope it will be of inspiration to anyone who is going through a difficult time in life's rich tapestry, that you can heal yourself.

And, I hope it has helped any reader know that even in the darkest of life's caves, there are, when you look luminescent creatures, which light up the way for you, bringing fun, laughter and adventure into the darkness. When it's light look for rainbows and when it's dark look for stars. You can heal yourself and others... if I can do it ... trust me ... anyone can. If you want to make a business out of it you can but if you just want to learn for your own sake as I have done, then that's perfectly OK too. Light and Love xxx Head towards the light ... it is there...trust me x

My Future

This Chapter is simply aimed at anyone who has lost a loved one, a main stay and has had to sort things out try to rebalance a family in light plus learn to love themselves. Taking time to rebuild yourself and family is important.

When my dad's brother dies, there is I believe, according to my uncle's family research, only one person in the world who holds my Father's family surname. The family name is a dying one. But, hopefully when that family name is no more those holding it or those apart of it will send it to the light well. I am part of that name.

It is in my heart and soul and spirit. I do things unreservedly, I have fun, I have adventures, I drift into things; and I know I am going back into the light. "I am going back into the light" is the most important part sentence I have ever written as for a short time recently I just closed down. Now I am opening up again as a new flower in the sun light.

But, how do I go back into the light? To simply have an end goal or a dream.

My dream is to be that old lady who despite the odds that she is facing has light in her face, light in her soul and most importantly, light in the spirit. The reason is that there is another whole layer, who has unconditional love to pave the way to the next life platform.... whatever it holds before my life here on Earth ends, and the semblance of my Father's name ends.

I dream and work for the hope that I leave this life as someone who had light and love in her face despite what she faced. I thank my yoga teacher, that she gave me the tools to breathe and to bend so I would not break and I am grateful to Tina, for giving me space to heal; and I bow down to the Universe and trust. And, really that's all I have to say, and I hope it helps someone who reads it this Chapter.

AUTHOR BIO

LAURA SHAWYER

Laura Shawyer is a women leaving her fabulous fifties decade and embarking on her new diamond decade where she is going to dream big and shine bright.

She is an independent lady who lives by the sea which she loves. She works as a Tor Manager, taking people on holiday and works on a marine conservation project in addition to teaching on the foreshore of the River Thames.

Laura is a healer, a Usui Reiki Master and Angelic Reiki Practitioner and has completed her Theta Training.

She contributes to Reiki Shares and has held space in an Angelic Reiki attunement. In her work to heal herself, she has been on retreats and workshops to support her growth and self-healing.

She believes that when the darker strands of life's rich tapestry happen in your life, you can heal yourself using different healing modalities which suit your needs thus avoiding the anti-depressant or sleeping pills route. She is an advocate of natural healing and self-soothing.

As she has healed, she is considering her future, and her end goal is to simply be a happy and free loving spirit. She is becoming interested in supporting others in their work to promote the spiritual path and to assist when the Universe gives her the opportunity to do so.

Contact

Email –laura.shawyer@hotamail.co.uk

RENE BOZIER

*S*o, there I was sitting in the car, wow what just happened?

I had just signed up for a homeopathy course; I had not expected that this morning. So there I was on the next part of my journey.

As far back as I can remember I felt different, I didn't feel like a child, I could never understand why children did silly things. I had toys and particularly a doll, Jimmy, he was my baby, he went everywhere with me, I still have him now in a box somewhere. I always needed to care for something.

That was my path in life. I never understood the way people did things that hurt others, but I got hurt, lots, so I built my glass wall, no one was going to get too close. I would care for others, but I would also look after myself.

My parents split up when I was about 10, divorcing on my 15th birthday. There had been lots of arguments, not usually in front of me, but my mother was very loud. She had me when she was just 17 so very young. She had a few jobs, then decided to go to college where she did her O levels, A levels, a Degree, started primary school teaching, then a social worker, then a probation officer, never really having a job, just an eternal student. My disabled Grandmother lived near us, then with us, and my mother became her carer.

My mother had quite a few men friends, some who were violent. I am not sure what was going on with her but I felt she didn't like me very much. She became an alcoholic who would take regular overdoses. I would come home from school and there she would be on the sofa with bottles of sherry and paracetamols. She was definitely on a path of self destruction.

There were many times she did strange things – she would drag me by my hair from parties with my friends, getting in by threatening their parents. When I look back, she was still young and had no support looking after 2 kids.

My dad had gone to work abroad, he earnt lots of money and would come back every 6 months and spend money on us, so we would have this weird life of eating in posh restaurants then going back to tinned spaghetti or burgers and chips for 5 months. My mums speciality was spaghetti bolognaise made with tinned mince, tinned tomatoes and tinned spaghetti.

I would push people away, if my own mother didn't love me how could I trust anyone else? I had a 'best friend' and then get upset if she would be friendly to others. It was easier to be friends with boys; they were so much simpler to understand.

My grandfather was my rock; he was solid, and I would stay with him at weekends. We would travel around London on buses, on the tube and on foot and he would teach me about London. My nan taught me some cooking skills.

I went to a Girls Grammar school but didn't like it; they all had their parents, lived in a house with a garden and spoke properly. (The perceptions of a teenager!!). I could not wait to leave school. Then I went to college to retake my O levels – this was the best thing ever, now I had fun, I enjoyed learning, these people were like me.

I wanted to take A levels but my mum was at University again so she needed me to go to work as she could not afford to pay the bills. Before I left college I met my husband to be – I was 17 he was 21. I left college and got a job,

We just knew we were going to be together, at 18 we bought a house, I remember going into estate agents and asking for their cheapest house – A 2 up, 2 down in 1980 for £16,999 with an interest rate of 15%. It was hard but we made our little home, had a camping cooker and a bucket of cold water for the fridge. We gradually got all the bits we needed. We got married in 1981 when I was 19.

We had our first child, a daughter when I was 21, life was good. While pregnant my mum had said – don't you dare ask me to babysit. So no support there then! When my daughter was about a year old, my uncle tried to 'take advantage' of me, although I was strong and made it clear I was not interested, I told my mother, who did not believe me, she chose him over me.

Why did she not love me? Was I really unlovable? That makes it very difficult to build relationships when the person who is meant to love you unconditionally doesn't love you. My glass wall around me became higher and stronger.

We did the house up and sold it for a profit then moved to a 3 bedroom house. My next door neighbour was a soft furnishing teacher, the class had a crèche – so began my love of soft furnishing. I took my qualifications, became a teacher and started my own very successful business. I had my son and we moved again to a village in Kent.

I had severe postnatal depression, it was not recognised until my son was 18 months old, this put a huge strain on everything. When it was recognised, I thought I was mad, I was working continually, but not coping with normal life, the GP was amazing and helped me recover without having to go into hospital.

We continued to buy houses that needed renovation, living in them with the kids, cats and dogs. Renovating them, then selling them on and buying another. We moved back to London so I had the support of friends. I had my 2nd daughter, life was good. I continued my business but was still studying.

I then began teaching interior design. I just knew there was something else, I didn't know what it was I just felt 'I was not quite there'. I went on so many training courses, but it just wasn't it – not what I was looking for. I then had my 4th child. We moved again this time to a wonderful huge Victorian house. I loved that house.

My business was really successful, we went on holidays, would eat out. But I felt something was still missing. Then my eldest became then pregnant at 17, having my grandson when she was only 2 weeks past her 18th birthday – I was with her at the birth.

THAT WAS IT!!!! I'd found it I wanted to be a midwife – I was 39, I was going to be a midwife!

I applied to university, I was successful, I started the training........ and I hated it. I could not understand why such a caring profession had so many people who didn't care. Why was it that I felt I needed to care? I needed to 'mother' others the way I had not been, it is a much safer way to do it, I cannot be hurt if I am the carer.

Women were shouted at to be quiet, left with their partner in the labour room scared. I was told not to stay in the room with them. When women came in with birth plans they would be laughed at in the coffee room. It was awful, and I could not be part of this conveyor belt.

There were the few wonderful midwives who continued the struggle to keep normality – as students we would fight to be with those few amazing midwives, but we couldn't all be with them. I loved working in the community, I could educate the women, help them to help themselves. Every year at university we had to do an elective placement, I chose to work with an Independent Midwife. That was the turning point – this was midwifery, continuity of care, real with woman caring and I loved it.

So that was my plan – I was going to be an Independent Midwife (IM). During the rest of my course I studied hard, I didn't care about epidurals, sections etc, obviously I had to be involved and know what I was doing, but I also knew that was not what I would be doing, so it wasn't so bad.

I just had to help the women understand what was happening and why – not which instrument the Doctor needed in theatre. I attended a couple of homebirths with the IM, the women had met me and invited me to their birth, what a privilege, I will never forget those births.

During this time my marriage broke down and I went through a divorce. I was studying for midwifery and continuing to make soft furnishings to pay the bills. Oh, and looking after the kids. Luckily, I had some amazing friends and my daughter who had moved out with her boyfriend was helping me with school runs and childcare.

There were times when I really didn't think it would ever be okay again. The university were really not very helpful, the hospital shift patterns were breaking me. I would be given shifts with hardly any notice and be expected to have childcare. Then write an essay during yet another argument. No one said it would be easy! Who wants an easy life?

Being an Independent Midwife was the best job ever in the whole world. I was in charge of my own caseload, I could chose to have time off (just not book anyone due at that time), the money was good. It was hard of course, I was on call 24/7, but it's different, I would only get called if there was a problem and the parents (to be) were worried, or it was time for a birth.

I would be as excited as them, well maybe not quite. I had a case-load of about 18 families in a year. I would become part of their family, some I have been midwife to the extended family – I would be known by all the family. That's how it should be, that very special time in a woman's life is extraordinary, but it is also completely ordinary, it is a normal physiological process which usually just needs support and encouragement.

Yes sometimes women need help, but amazingly women were built to birth, it is usually – too much 'help' that ruins a totally good experience. As my children grew up and had their own babies, I was midwife to them, having wonderful home water births, what a brilliant start to their parenting lives and truly unmediated start for the babies.

I had joined the IM who I had my work experience with, she was the best teacher. I took on high risk women in my first year, under her guidance; I had 2 sets of twins, a lady with epilepsy, another with gestational diabetes, another with extreme fear of birth, among others.

This is the best way to learn as it is real, they all had hospital births with me supporting them alongside the hospital team

(IM's cannot work in hospital, although there are a couple of exceptions). The lady with birth fear had a home birth, my first as a first midwife, on my birthday. It was the most empowering, amazing thing I had done for anyone, she overcame all her fears (of everything) and became a strong courageous women. If I had never facilitated another birth, all my training would have been worth it for that.

I worked with the midwife for 2 years, she then retired and handed me her business, how much better can life get. A student came out with me as I had done with my mentor. When she qualified, she joined me, we were a great team, we loved working together, we became and still are great friends.

Then we had another student who also joined us once she qualified. She has had both her babies with us since. I remarried. All was going well, until my husband was made redundant from a well-paid job. He became depressed; I could not afford my wonderful Victorian house any more so we had to sell. We moved into a much smaller house but it was lovely too.

As IM's we did not need insurance, we were (and still are) well-regulated and as long as it was explained to the parents about the insurance, we can still be struck off the register for negligence but as IM's we are there, putting the woman at the centre of her care, so negligence is unlikely to be an issue.

The family also interviews the midwife so would only book her if they felt a bond. Then in about 2010, the European Union decided we would need insurance – but it was not available anywhere. This meant we would have to stop working in October 2013.

That was a huge blow to us and the families we care for. Some of my friends who were also IM's had got together and formed Neighbourhood Midwives (NM) this was a huge project, but they did get insurance. I was their first employed midwife.

I was in a group of the most amazing women, who were also midwives; we had the same philosophy of care. It was great, there were some issues of course, I needed to have more clients, less money, more travel. But we were a team, we had meetings that were incredibly supportive, training days geared at homebirths.

NM were trying to get contracts in the NHS, alongside the private side, so things became more rigid, but we were taken seriously by hospitals, they had heard of us, not like as an IM where I felt like I had 3 heads at times. My friend left NM, I had another midwife buddy who I love but she also left, then another, this way of working is not for everyone. I began to feel unsupported, in many ways but still overall supported.

The births that were in hospital or where mothers needing to be transferred in needed my support, but I wasn't getting the back up support. The more intervention in hospital the harder the birth is, there is so much unnecessary intervention I was finding it really hard to cope with this, it seemed every hospital birth was ending in a medical birth with antibiotics for mum and or baby.

Surely every women can't need them. I did lots of research and was finding it so difficult to be positive with women who were accepting them on advice from doctors but not questioning, then those who did question were scared as the threat of a dead baby is so hard to ignore.

Inductions of labour – without good reason, were becoming more common. I was finding this very difficult to cope with. Being positive for the woman and supporting them and then the doctor overruling when I had worked so hard on giving evidence based care. I was becoming low, I think my get up and go had got up and gone. I could not support women when I was empty. I needed to rethink what I was doing.

I still loved the homebirths, but if I chose just home birth support I was not giving choice to women. Yes they could choose another midwife but not when one is not available in the area. After 11 years of midwifery I decided to look at other ways of helping people. Again I started on the courses. I had done lots of short homeopathy courses, to help during labour and the postnatal time and Bush flower essences.

I was thinking about my retirement, I would not be able to do the long labours, stuck in ridiculous positions for hours on end for many more years. I was seeing an osteopath monthly to put my back, back into place, but how long could that go on for?

I loved homeopathy, seeing a homeopath for myself and my children as I did not want to use antibiotics on them, I looked into a few courses, but they were difficult to do alongside midwifery. I could not stop working I had to earn money.

I looked at online courses, but I'm not good with self –motivation.

I used the yellow birth box remedies at labours and was amazed at the results. I really wanted to take this further, I would not have to be on call, I could do it from anywhere in the world. We were planning on moving to the West Country to escape London, this was perfect. I just needed to find out how to do it...... Then the telephone call came.

I was sitting in my car having just finished an appointment for one of my midwifery clients, a homeopath colleague called to ask me a midwifery question as she sometimes did. I hadn't really told her about my plans. We chatted and she said 'I don't know why you don't train to be a homeopath you would be really good at it' my answer – I would love to but can't find a course.

She said 'wait there I will call you back in 10 mins' she did, her friend runs a homeopathic college one weekend a month, not too far from me; a 3 year course ending in being a licenced homeopath. She gave me her details – I called her, within 10 mins of a fluke telephone call I was signed up to a homeopathy course that was to change my life AGAIN.

I did not want to stop being a midwife, I am very proud of it, but I just don't like the system. So to be a homeopath too I would be able to help in other ways, the perfect combination. Plus I would be able to help the wider family. I had run businesses, I have many past clients, how hard could it be? Homeopathy is just giving a little white sugar pill that performs miracles, is it not?

I truly believe the universe has mapped out a path for each of us, we just have to be open to it. I was meant to have the mother I had - to make me seek help, to make me stronger. To love my granddad to make me see I could love that much, I was not numb. I was meant to be a mother with the experiences I had, miscarriage, a baby with issues at birth who needed operations and long term appointments, the threat of a caesarean, an induced birth, severe postnatal depression.

To have a difficult child where I needed every ounce of my being to try and help – although I feel I failed terribly at that, but that, now, I also believe was/is a lesson. I am working on myself with the help of my homeopath to clear something that we believe he was here to teach me. Having so many life experiences has made me who I am, I have to be grateful for that.

Another of my paths was my marriages, my first husband was a great dad, supporting me in the way I wanted to bring them up, opposite to how my mother treated me. We worked well together, renovating houses, supporting me in my quest for whatever it was that I was trying to find.

But after 25 years it was no longer working. Strangely, my now husband must have crossed my path many times, we had gone to the same places when I was at school and college, but we never met. We had to meet when the time was right, it was because he earnt enough money to pay the bills it allowed me to become an IM.

I was successful, so once he was made redundant I could keep us going for a while. He has been fundamental in my journey, supporting me in whatever I decide to do, picking me up at all hours from hospitals when I have had to transfer a woman in via ambulance. I still have my glass wall, I cannot let it go completely, I want to but I cannot be hurt, I cannot totally trust.

I started my homeopathy course, I had met my tribe in my class-mates, it felt like it was just meant to be, we all helped each other, from different walks of life. I loved it. No pressure, other than from ourselves. During the first year I was going to heal the world, why didn't everyone use it? The second year I could see how powerful this stuff is, the 3rd year is scary, if it can do so much good, could it do harm with the wrong remedy.

I had some advantage that as with midwifery you cannot help someone who does not want to be helped, the client has to come to you. The course was about each of us as individuals, we learnt to meditate, to do journey work, to see ourselves as part of the bigger picture, it started to make sense in one way but became more confusing in another.

What was my purpose? I was a good midwife, so did I have the right to stop, there may have been many more families who needed me, who I could make a difference to, but what about me? I was becoming broken, I had to consider that too.

Then as I learnt more about the natural way of living I could not be part of the Health service, antibiotics 'just in case' without a thought for the future. The number of vaccines that are being given to babies, without informed consent, withholding knowl-edge from the parents, if there is nothing to hide, why hide the information.

I was becoming so disillusioned with society. My midwifery colleagues and fellow homeopaths were my tribes, and I felt safe with them, what is happening to make people so coercive in the pharmaceutical industry? Are we really scaring them that they have to put up such a one sided fight? More confusion.

With the 'Bigger Plan' the universe had for me I was confused; do I do homeopathy? Do I move away? Do I continue midwifery? I had a pretty hard time with the midwifery, all the things I dislike in the system kept being repeated. I needed to make some decisions.

Neighbourhood Midwives went into liquidation – a total shock, with only one weeks' notice for us all, well that was a pretty big sign! I had loads of homework to do for my homeopathy course to graduate but never had the time to do it, I was so busy midwifery wise, but now I had time.

A bit drastic but I was able to catch up with everything to be able to graduate. Most of the NM midwives continued to care for the women who had booked our care, they had already paid, so we did it for no pay. Each time I thought I would not be able to pay my mortgage something turned up.

I took more courses to do with birth, I became a placenta encap-sulation specialist. 3 step rewind practitioner for birth trauma – this is so powerful, l have had some amazing results from women, men and midwives who have suffered PTSD trauma from birth. The Real Birth Company antenatal classes, all so I would be able to pick up work wherever I was.

I completed my homeopathy course and graduated, I have had some interesting cases, with some outstanding results. This has helped me to start the transition from midwife to homeopath; I'm still helping and caring for people.

While working and studying it was difficult to keep up with friends, I called a friend one evening and she said that Tina would be at hers the next week to do readings - I wanted to know what to do, with definitive answers. How brilliant that she was there as I wanted answers, I went along, and had my reading, there were many things that resonated for me.

She said my new venture would take off, she saw homeopathy but didn't understand as she knew I was a midwife. She had told me 2 years previously that I would move this year to the West Country. We were having lots of viewings on my house, but it was just not selling, was there a reason? Am I not meant to go yet? She helped me manifest selling and visualising my new home. In my previous reading with Tina she had felt I had many health issues with my pelvis, she was holding her stomach saying she could feel the pain.

I have had pelvic and sciatic problems since my second pregnancy. I had accepted it as just me. I had seen the GP many times as sometimes I could not cope with the pain. I was taking regular pain relief. Until 17 years later I had another issue and saw an osteopath, in one hour he changed my life, I was free of pain. That was the beginning of my journey with alternative/complimentary health care.

The previous week I had an awful cough, using my remedies was helping, but it just kept changing. I had been at college over that weekend and taken a remedy, the cough stopped but then I had a pain in my head, not a headache but almost like lightening, I thought it must be a trapped nerve from the coughing.

That week it got worse to the point I could not concentrate, it was awful, I called all my osteopath friends to get an appointment. I saw one and she improved it for about an hour. It was connected to my pelvis again! With the manipulation I felt the pain in my pelvis too. I turned to allopathic drugs; I just could not deal with the pain.

Over that weekend I took medication and felt at least human, on the Sunday my friend called and said Tina had text her to say she was doing Angelic healing on Monday and to call me (I had not mentioned my head pain to her). I went along thinking it's worth a go, I was willing to try anything to stop this pain. Thirty minutes of treatment with the Angels and feeling some very odd things going on around my solar plexus, the pain had gone – and has not come back.

As mentioned earlier I have been seeing a homeopath for many years, starting for my daughter who had psoriasis, my son had recurring tonsillitis and I had eczema, all improved with the remedies. That homeopath was reducing her work load to stop practicing. During my studies we had a tutor who I just knew had to be my homeopath, she lives quite a distance from me but I felt a connection and she was the one to help with the deeper issues I had.

She works spiritually and feels my pelvis issues are from a previous life, my sons and my souls, had a pact that they would be here to help me resolve those issues, it would not be easy, it hasn't!!! We have been working on that, I have also had time to be kinder to myself, remembering I have had osteopathy monthly for 7 or 8 years so I can continue to be a midwife – I get into some pretty weird positions being a home birth midwife – the osteopathy always helps but does not hold.

For the last 7 months I have been seeing my osteopath, homeopath and have now started Pilates. I have felt huge improvement; my pelvis is not my main thought of the day anymore. I also feel differently about life. Is my glass wall being removed block by block?

I am not worried that I cannot sell my house, if I am meant to go I will, the perfect home will be available at that time, if I am meant to stay here there is a reason.

When I realised that, I said I would only take midwifery clients that had had a homebirth with me before, within one hour I had a text from a previous client. Since then two more home birth clients have contacted me. I am also taking on homeopathy clients with amazing results.

The universe has her plan, I am listening.

Hello@ReneBozier.com

www.RENEBOZIER.com

AUTHOR BIO

RENE BOZIER

Rene Bozier is a midwife and homeopath. She has lived in London all her life with a short time in Kent. She has 4 children, 13 Grandchildren, 3 step children and 1 Great granddaughter.

Rene has always had dogs and cannot imagine life without them. Rene likes to travel but equally likes to be at home.

Rene had a difficult childhood, her parents' marriage breakdown in her early teens meant living with her alcoholic and unstable mother, who she now realises, was probably having a mental breakdown. This caused problems at school and stopped Rene from having a childhood, although her Grandfather was the stability in her life.

Rene bought her first house at 18, married at 19 and had her first daughter at 21, having a son at 23, another daughter at 28 and her 2nd son at 31.

Rene started going to Adult education classes to learn soft furnishing, turning this into a very successful business, qualifying with City and Guilds to become an Adult Education teacher. Loving learning and teaching she went onto become an Interior Design and soft furnishing teacher.

After having her children and being at the birth of her first grand-child Rene decided to train as a midwife. During training Rene went through a marriage breakdown and divorce, also continuing to make curtains to make ends meet.

Training was not as expected, Rene could not understand how such a caring profession felt very conveyor belt and uncaring. When she discovered Independent Midwifery she never looked back.

While being an Independent Midwife Rene has continued in her studies, learning many extra skills, basic homeopathy, hypno-birthing, rebozo, reiki, Bush flower remedies; anything that can make birth easier for her clients.

Rene enjoys the trusting relationship she builds with her clients, looking after them through the pregnancy, birth and 6 weeks postnataly. She has some clients who have had 3 babies with her, then been invited to naming ceremonies, christenings, weddings, becoming part of the family.

Rene married again to an incredibly supportive husband who has helped her grow as a midwife, he would be there to pick her up in the middle of the night from different hospitals after she had supported women through their birth.

Rene has been midwife to six of her grandchildren, having home births, resulting in very special relationships with them.

Rene after 12 years on call 24/7 for her Independent clients decided to train to be a homeopath, alongside continuing with midwifery. Three years of training and now qualified. Rene is now only taking a few midwifery clients and concentrating on homeopathy and the other spiritual skills learnt whilst being a midwife.

During the Homeopathy journey, Rene has grown spiritually, understanding more about herself and her upbringing, no longer upset with it but realising it was her journey and she needed to make it to be the person she is today.

hello@renebozier.com

www.ReneBozier.com (this is not up and running yet)

Printed in Poland
by Amazon Fulfillment
Poland Sp. z o.o., Wrocław